shewill

anchor deep

52-Week Devotionals

Created by

The *shewill* Conference

Leadership Team

Aaron Publishing
Lyles, TN 37098
www.aaronpublishing.com

First Printing October 2022

ISBN-:978-0-9989385-7-8

Printed in the United States of America

Foreword

Dear Sister,

We are so excited to share with you our first collaborative writing project. Our prayer is that this devotional will be used in such a way that your relationship with Christ will be significantly different than when you first started. Whether you choose to use this book as a 52-week tool or a 52-day tool, we know that God is going to meet with you. Look up the scriptures in your bible, try different translations, read the verse above and the verse below, follow the prompting of the Holy Spirit and dig deeper in the verses He is highlighting to you. There is a place after each devotional for you to respond to God. Do not forsake this! This is your linger lounge time. Spend at least 5 minutes daily lingering in the presence of the Lord and listen to Him speak to you. Write down everything that comes to mind, prayers, scriptures, ideas, thoughts. At the end of the 52 devotionals look back and see what is the main idea that the Lord is saying to you in this season. He may just blow your socks off!

As you work through this devotional book, you will come to know each member of the She Will Team more intimately as you read their stories, their thoughts, and as they share God's Word with you. Each woman reveals their own personality through their writings. Some will do more teaching while others exercise their gift of encouragement. This book is an example of the Body of Christ working together to benefit the whole. It is absolutely beautiful!

Let me introduce you to some of my best friends, my sisters. Between these pages you will meet:

Victoria Steelman, our Development Director, and Speaker. She is a lover of all things Jesus and that includes His people. She does all the things, team photographer, hair stylist, songwriter, singer, and connector of dots!

Kelly Levatino, our Marketing Director, and Speaker. She has a sarcastic sense of humor that is weaved throughout her Spiritual teachings, and she is always as cool as a cucumber. May try Stand-Up soon!

Savanna Holubec, our Merchandiser/Buyer, and occasional Speaker. She is highly creative and is carrying on her Lovey's Legacy of Love. Also, very sarcastic and one of the offspring of Shelsea.

Sara Prather, our Prayer Director, and occasional Speaker. She knows how to war in the spirit realm and will be your battle buddy. Know this, she is praying for you!

Liz Catlin, our Hello Hard Gal and Speaker. She is a lover of words and especially the Word. She talks a mile a minute and will talk about Jesus all day long!

Thresa Lawson, our Team Mentor and Speaker. She is on fire for Jesus, has the best advice, and loves with every ounce of herself. If she is awake, she is moving!

Julie West, Speaker and a biblical scholar who brings us straight into the Jewish culture to get a more immersed understanding of the scriptures. She loves digging into the deeper meaning and sharing it with us!

Bev McCann, our Multimedia Producer and Speaker. She carries a bucket of joy around and gives it away for free, kind of like confetti. She sprinkles kindness everywhere she goes!

Dawn Wendel, our Hospitality Director and maybe one day a future Speaker. She is as compassionate as you can get and can feel others' emotions as if they were hers. She intercedes on your behalf. She also loves all things cheetah print!

Laura Anne Smith, our Registration Director. She is detail oriented, laughs with ease, and makes everyone around her feel incredibly welcomed. She asks all the right questions and does a lot of the thinking for us!

Joy Roe, Mentor to Shelsea. She equips those who are called into ministry all over the world. She is in her seventies and very comfortable holding us to accountability as she prays over this team daily.

Jo Ann McComack, our FUNdraiser and a woman with the best servant heart. She is a helper no matter what is asked. She is passionate about Jesus, Kingdom work, and always looks to find the good within everyone. She also always looks good!

Then there is me, Shelsea, Founder, Speaker, Host. I am the one God tapped on the shoulder to bring this conference to fruition. I live in what we call the "God Zone". Meaning nothing I do can be done by me but only by HE!

Truthfully, we have all been tapped by God to do the role He has asked us to do. As you can see, a "me" calling can only be fulfilled in a "we" context. We need each other. I need these women. I am blessed to call them my sisters.

They are now your sisters too!

Anchor Deep,

Shelsea

Proclamation

When you feel adrift…**Anchor Deep**

When uncertainties arise…**Anchor Deep**

When navigating decisions…**Anchor Deep**

When the storms of life come…**Anchor Deep**

When you feel dry and thirsty…**Anchor Deep**

When peace is what you yearn for…**Anchor Deep**

When you feel like you are drowning in shame…**Anchor Deep**

When the only thing that will satisfy is His presence…**Anchor Deep**

When you are being tossed about like a boat out to sea…**Anchor Deep**

Where she drops her anchor matters. Will she **ANCHOR DEEP** in the Word of God? Will she

SOAK in the presence of God? Will she quench her **THIRST** by drinking Living Water? Will she

allow the grace of Christ to **CLEANSE** her? Will she dive deep and **IMMERSE** herself into all that God has for her?

SHE WILL

Week 1

Hebrews 6:19 NIV

"We have this hope as an anchor for the soul, firm and secure."

We have all heard the verse, the scripture that says" We have this hope as an anchor for the soul, firm and secure". We've seen it written in beautiful calligraphy and put on walls and signs but what does it really mean to have this hope as an anchor for our soul? Where are we to set anchor? How do we set our anchor in "this hope"? What is "this hope"?

Hope sometimes can feel like a balloon wavering in the wind but this is not what "this hope" is talking about. It's not "I hope you have a good day," "I hope this turns out well," or "I hope these pants fit." That is not the hope that we are going to set our anchor in. That kind of hope is like being tossed about on a boat at sea.

No, the kind of hope we will set our anchor in is confidently knowing that when we put our trust in Christ Jesus, that God's promises will not fail. God's promises are backed up by God's oath. God has made a covenant with His people; a contract that cannot be broken. Set your anchor deep in "this hope". The promises of God are backed by the sovereignty of God. God is saying "I promise on myself that my promises are unfailing, and they will come to pass". How do we know the promises will come to pass? We've seen God do it and we know that Jesus Christ is the same yesterday and today and forever! (Hebrews 13:8) God will do what He says He will do! Consider it done.

All throughout scripture we can find evidence of God promising and then fulfilling. We read in the book of Genesis about the Abrahamic Covenant where God gave Abraham a promise that he would be a father to many nations, he would be blessed and multiplied. God fulfilled His promise with the birth of Issac. In the first four books of the New Testament, we witness different accounts of the same promise being fulfilled by the New Covenant. That promise was spoken of first in Jeremiah 31:31-33. God promised us a Savior, one who could take away sin, reconcile us back to our Heavenly Father and give us the gift of eternal life. God fulfilled His promise through His son Christ Jesus. Then we see Christ promise that when He goes to the Father, He will send us the Holy Spirit. (John 16:7) We see evidence of this fulfillment daily with God's people.

Will She anchor in the hope that comes from the Lord?
Will She anchor deep?
She Will!

Lord, thank you that I can trust your word and your promises. I place my hope in you and you alone. Forgive me for my unbelief and stir up faith within me, that I can walk in confidence of who you are, knowing that your promises are yes and Amen.

Shelsea

Your Thoughts….

Will She Anchor Deep?

I will anchor deep in trusting God with our future as we grow older. I will anchor deep in believing my kids will follow you and return to you when they fall away. Your word does not return void and they know your word and your ways. It is in them - still. Your word anchors deep in their heart + soul.

…. shewill!!!

Week 2

Jeremiah 29:11 NIV

"For I know the plans I have for you," declares the LORD, "plans to prosper you and not to harm you, plans to give you hope and a future."

God is the creator of the universe. He created the stars, the skies, the oceans, and everything else that is magnificent. Then he created humanity; He created you and me.

God created everything to have a purpose. We were created on purpose for a purpose. Since "God created man in his own image" (Gen. 1:27a), we must have significance. We are a special part of creation. We were designed to communicate with God.

God calls us by name. He wants to be in a relationship with you. He made you in His likeness. God makes it evident that He cares about us, for He has known us since we were still in the womb (see Jer. 1:5). He even knows the number of hairs on our heads (see Luke 12:7)!!

This proves that God doesn't just flippantly create and then leave the creation.

By believing God chose to create us as we are, we can anchor in the confidence that God is in control. As Jeremiah 29:11 states, God has a plan for each one of His children. He plans to prosper you. God is a God of hope, light, and joy. He wants you to be able to experience those attributes.

God knows you. When you feel hopeless, you must lean back on these truths. There is a reason and a plan for your life. Do not lose hope. The future is bright, especially the eternal future-Heaven with Jesus!

What truths are you anchoring in?

Will She anchor deep into God's truths about her life?

She Will!!!

Dear Heavenly Father,

Thank you for intentionally pursuing me. Thank you for knowing me. Thank you that you have a plan of hope for me. May I lean on you when I feel as if despair is overwhelming my soul? Be the ruler of my life. Lead me. Guide me. Amen.

Savanna

Your Thoughts....

Will She Anchor Deep?

_____
_____
_____
_____
_____
_____
_____
_____
_____
_____
_____
_____
_____
_____
_____
_____

.... _shewill!!!_

Week 3

Ezekiel 36:25 NIV

"I will sprinkle clean water on you, and you will be clean; I will cleanse you from all your impurities and from all your idols."

Do you remember the day you came to believe in our Lord Jesus? That beautiful refreshing moment when you prayed to receive salvation through your faith in God's son. Just like that you felt lighter, like a ton of bricks was taken off your chest! For me it was the most refreshing moment of my life!

Like a shower cleanses us on the outside, we are eternally clean on the inside. His sacrifice was enough to make us like new!

We now are filled with God's Spirit, The Holy Spirit! That same spirit that raised Christ from the dead now lives in us to purify us and empower us every moment of every day, for the rest of our lives to help us overcome this world!

Those we read about in the Old Testament did not have that same blessing, the struggle had to be real! They had the promise but not the fulfillment, that did not come for 400 years after the last book of the Old Testament.

Today we have been given a magnificent gift and we must not take it for granted.

We must remember we can and will overcome this world with the power of The Holy Spirit if we allow Him to help us!

Are you allowing The Lord to cleanse you today?

Will She be cleansed?

She Will!

Dear Lord Thank you for dying for my sins, cleanse me of anything that I have done to dishonor your sacrifice. Give me your strength through the power of The Holy Spirit today to live a life worthy of your love, while I know there is nothing, I can do to earn my salvation, let everything I do today honor you and your love for me.

In Christ Name

Victoria

Your Thoughts....

Will She Anchor Deep?

_____
_____
_____
_____
_____
_____
_____
_____
_____
_____
_____
_____
_____
_____
_____
_____
_____
_____

.... shewill!!!

Week 4

Isaiah 1:18 NLT

"Come now, let's settle this," says the LORD. "Though your sins are like scarlet, I will make them as white as snow; though they are red as crimson, they shall be like wool."

Isaiah conveyed this message from God to the Israelites when they were smack in the middle of total rebellion. Their hearts had completely turned away from God, but they continued to go through the motions of worshiping Him. God knew their hearts weren't in it, and He frankly told them to "stop bringing meaningless offerings!"

Yikes!

Turns out God can see straight into our hearts any time He wants to, and He isn't a fan of wrongly motivated "worship". Motivation always matters to God. The ends do not justify the means with Him.

It's easy for us to get in the routine of going to church, singing songs to and about God, and rarely thanking God for the food on our plates. But if our hearts aren't in it, if we aren't motivated by love for God–He doesn't want us to do these things.

We all find ourselves in spiritual ruts every now and then. The good news is we don't have to stay there! We simply have to tell God the truth–that we're just going through the motions–and then ask Him to renew a right spirit within us. And He will! (Maybe not immediately, but He will because it is a prayer that we know from scripture is in accordance with His will.)

This "coming back to Jesus" is exactly what God is talking about in this Isaiah verse. God is poised, ready to forgive Israel's sin of complacency. In the same way, He is ready to cleanse us from our sin of just going through the Christian motions.

If you are finding yourself less than thrilled about worship, church, prayer, or personal Bible study, God is saying to you, "Come now, let's settle this." Meet with Him and allow Him to make your sins white as snow, white as wool.

Will She let the Lord cleanse her sins away?

She Will!

Lord, thank you for consistently loving us, whether our hearts are excited about you or not. Even when we completely turn our backs on You, Your love drives You to pursue us still. Forgive us for our lackadaisical attitudes toward You. Renew a right spirit within us and help us to remember who You are and why You are worthy of our praise. We receive the washing away of our sin of complacency You offer us. From this point on, help us move forward with renewed zeal for You, the Lord of Lords, the King of Kings, and the Redeemer of our souls through Christ Jesus!

Kelly

Your Thoughts….

Will She Anchor Deep?

_____

_____

_____

_____

_____

_____

_____

_____

_____

_____

_____

_____

_____

_____

.... shewill!!!

Week 5

Psalms 25:5 NIV

"Lead me in Your truth and teach me, For You are God of my salvation; On You I will wait all the day."

Most of my prayers have this verse in it. All I want is to know God more and to know more about him. In reality Psalms 25:1-10 is just so beautifully written.

1| O LORD, I give my life to you. 2| I trust in you, my God! Do not let me be disgraced, or let my enemies rejoice in my defeat. 3| No one who trusts in you will ever be disgraced, but disgrace comes to those who try to deceive others. 4| Show me the right path, O LORD; point out the road for me to follow.

5| Lead me by your truth and teach me, for you are the God who saves me. All day long I put my hope in you. 6| Remember, O LORD, your compassion and unfailing love, which you have shown from long ages past. 7| Do not remember the rebellious sins of my youth. Remember me in the light of your unfailing love, for you are merciful, O LORD.

8| The LORD is good and does what is right; he shows the proper path to those who go astray.

9| He leads the humble in doing right, teaching them his way. 10| The LORD leads with unfailing love and faithfulness all who keep his covenant and obey his demands.

Was there ever a time you felt defeated, deceived, rebelled? These verses tell us we no longer need to feel that way. Give your life to Him. Seek him. Anchor with Him. Linger with him. Be obedient to Him. It spells it all out right here. God's hope is yours; God's compassion, unfailing love and faithfulness is right there for you if we keep his covenant and obey his demands.

Father, just like this verse says, lead me in your truth and teach me. I want nothing more than to be more like you. I am blessed that you never left me. I am blessed for all of your compassion, faithfulness and unfailing love in Jesus' name, Amen.

Will She anchor deep in the word of God?

She Will!

Dawn

Your Thoughts….

Will She Anchor Deep?

_____

_____

_____

_____

_____

_____

_____

_____

_____

_____

_____

_____

_____

_____

.... shewill!!!

Week 6

Matthew 3:6 NIV

"Confessing their sins, they were baptized by him in the Jordan River."

When Jesus walked the earth, three things were required of someone wanting to convert to Judaism: baptism, circumcision, and sacrifice. Legendary rabbi Hillel, who lived about the time of Jesus, insisted baptism, which Judaism calls tvilah, was more important than even circumcision, because it symbolized washing sins away. Baptism/Tvilah is still a part of their conversion process today. Even then, baptism was not the redemptive act, but a symbol of it.

In Matthew 3, no one, not even religious leaders, challenged the young prophet baptizing. They may have doubted their own need for immersion, but no one suggested there was anything unusual or heretical about the act of baptism itself. In Acts 8, the Ethiopian eunuch reading Isaiah knew about baptism. 2 Chronicles 4:2 provides the dimensions of a tank for ceremonial cleansing. The pools of Siloam and Bethsaida were used for a similar purpose.

To understand our passage, we must know; who was the "him" doing the baptizing? On the surface, the answer is obviously John the Baptist. More importantly, Matthew 3:3 reveals that John was the one prophesied in Isaiah 40:3 "who makes straight the way of the Lord". Once people truly understand John's purpose, it cannot be denied; Jesus is the Messiah, Mark 1:1-8, Matthew 3:11-16.

Matthew 3 is not simply a baptism story. It is a bold declaration that the Messiah had arrived.

By pointing to Isaiah 40, Matthew 3 reveals a Lord who comes in power, 2 Peter 1:16-21. It describes God walking through the towns of Judah, Luke 10:38, John11:54. It promises one who leads like a shepherd and holds His lambs near his heart, John 10:11. He is the God who is over creation, John 1. Could there be a clearer description of Jesus?

Today, baptism is the acknowledgement our hearts have been circumcised, Deuteronomy 30:6, Romans 2:28-29. It is an active confession that Jesus was the ultimate sacrifice Hebrews 10:10, and our sins have been washed away, Acts 22:16. It is our declaration Jesus is the Messiah!

Will She declare Jesus is the Messiah?

She Will!

Lord, what do I have without you? You provide everything I need and blessings I do not deserve. Keep me from callousness. Keep sin far from me. And keep me from drifting from you. Let me be a John the Baptist to this generation. May I always make it easier for others to understand who You are and what you have done for all of us. Never let me take your love for granted. Make me mindful of your holiness in all I do. May I never grow tired of declaring,

"Jesus is the Messiah!"

Julie

Your Thoughts....

Will She Anchor Deep?

_____

_____

_____

_____

_____

_____

_____

_____

_____

_____

_____

_____

_____

_____

_____

_____

.... *shewill!!!*

Week 7

Hebrews 10:23 NLT

"Let us hold tightly without wavering to the hope we affirm, for God can be trusted to keep his promise."

By the time Captain Dawn Riley stepped aboard the newly renamed Heineken, the boat was the only thing not sinking. The all-female crew's morale had bottomed out long before Captain Dawn received an urgent request to take the helm of the sailboat and help salvage its arduous race around the world in the 1993-94 Whitbread Round-the-world race.

The crew, under Captain Dawn's leadership, endured many difficult and life-threatening situations in the 32,000 miles it traveled... but physical injuries, dwindling supplies, and faulty equipment were nothing compared to the building resentment, both on water and land, stemming from controversy over the recruitment of the new leader. The harrowing tales of this fearless crew is chronicled in the book "Taking the Helm" by Dawn Riley.

One can most certainly understand the crews cause for concern; after only four days of preparation, this leader they were unsure of, now holds their lives in balance by the decisions she makes. Their only hope was that this Captain was prepared and proven. Thankfully, we have a leader at the helm that has more than proven His ability to steer our lives in all kinds of treacherous situations.

It is when we trust God to hold tightly to the helm as we hold tightly to Him, that we find we can circumnavigate this life with ease. Isaiah 43:2 says it best I think... "When you pass through the waters, I will be with you; and when you pass through the rivers, they will not sweep over you." NLT

This scripture is one of over 7500 promises of God in His Word. It's in the hope of each of these that we can say without fear "There isn't an area of my life, no storm, no challenge, nothing...that God can't sail through, and I can't weather with Him at the helm."

Who's at the helm of your life?

Will She hold tight?

She Will!

Heavenly Father, we are so thankful there is nothing in this life that you can't see us safely through; you make ways where there are no ways! Help us to hold tight to that truth...show us daily who is at the helm of our life and when it's not you, allow us quickly to recognize it so that we are not driven off course. Remind us often to rest in your promises according to your Word.

For it is in you we have the assurance of all things hoped for.

In Jesus name, Amen.

Liz

Your Thoughts….

Will She Anchor Deep?

_____

_____

_____

_____

_____

_____

_____

_____

_____

_____

_____

_____

_____

_____

_____

.... shewill!!!

Week 8

John 7:38 NLT

"Anyone who is thirsty may come to me! Anyone who believes in me may come and drink? For the scriptures declare, 'Rivers of living water will flow from his heart'."

In 2007, Dave Buschow died of thirst a mere 100 yards from water. On a wilderness survival adventure, Buschow and others sought to test their physical and mental endurance by hiking for miles drinking only what they could find from natural resources. On that fateful day, after nearly 10 hours without water, he became bleary eyed, delusional, and suffered slurred speech and cramping muscles; until he finally collapsed in the100 degree heat under the blazing Utah sun.

"It was so needless. What a shame. It didn't have to happen," said the Sheriff's department. [1]

How comparable this story is to us today who have a deep longing for something to satisfy the inner thirsting. We keep searching only to find satisfaction elusive. It is needless. It is a shame, and it doesn't have to be.

Many times, Jesus had witnessed the water libation ceremony (pouring out) recorded in John 7.

The priest would ceremoniously fill a golden vessel with "living water" from the pool of Siloam.

While he was on his way back to the temple platform, other priests would stand shoulder to shoulder moving their feet in unison, swishing the willow branches from side to side, making a 'rushing wind" sound. The flute player, or "pierced one" would then call for both wind and water to enter the temple. After the leaves had been shaken from the willow branches and the palms beaten in pieces, the priest would pray for rains to come and the Spirit to be poured out. [2]

Then, in a climactic jubilant act, with songs of Hallel being sung the priest would take the wine from the silver vessel and mix it with the "living water" and pour it out over the altar. [3]

This time though, as Jesus watched, something significant happened. Jesus knew the deep thirst experienced by so many who longed for a drink of living water. He knew the parched, dry souls that needed a cleansing. He also knew that very soon; the ceremony would become a reality in his life. He interrupts the pompous celebration, "Anyone who is thirsty may come to me!"

I hear Him calling out to you today.

Is anyone thirsty today?

Do you need a refreshing from the waters of life?

Will She come and be cleansed and refreshed?

She Will!

Jesus, today we answer your call. We recognize we are dry and parched and our soul is in need of cleansing. Come Lord Jesus, and wash us, cleanse us. Let us partake of the living water that we may never thirst again. Amen.

Thresa

[1] Dan, Glaister, "Hallucinating, vomiting and unable to stand, but guides refused water to dying trekker," TheGuardian.com., May 6, 2007.

https://www.theguardian.com/world/2007/may/07/usa.topstories3. accessed May 7, 2020.

[2] Perry Stone Hebraic Prophetic Study Bible, "John in Depth, The Feast of Tabernacles and the Last Day of the Feast; John 7, "Rivers of Living Water." Bible.org., Feb 9, 2014.

https://bible.org/seriespage/lesson-43-rivers-living-water-you-and-you-john-737-39, accessed, May 7, 2020.

[3] Derived from the Hebrew word, Halall, meaning 'praise.' In Jewish liturgical, Psalms 113-118, read on festive occasions such as the "Water Libation Ceremony".

Your Thoughts….

Will She Anchor Deep?

_____
_____
_____
_____
_____
_____
_____
_____
_____
_____
_____
_____
_____
_____
_____
_____
_____

.... shewill!!!

Week 9

John 3:5 NIV

"Jesus replied, "I assure you; no one can enter the Kingdom of God without being born of water and the Spirit."

Years ago, I wrote a song about this very thing titled, "Have You Been Born Again?" This passage in John is talking about being washed in the spirit of the Lord. This statement, "being born again" confused Nicodemus, and it might have you a little baffled.

Jesus told Nicodemus, no, you silly man, I'm not talking about re-entering the womb, I'm talking about something much greater; the power of the holy spirit to cleanse you within and wash you clean so that your spirit is born fresh and anew, your spirit will be born again.

Think of it like an old ringer washer. We need to submerge ourselves in the Love of God, allow Jesus to become Lord of our life, and accept Jesus as our Savior. We need to get into the washer of the Holy Spirit, and let the Holy Spirit do the work as we are soaking in the love of the Lord and getting cleansed of all the dirt in our lives, Reborn!

I say we, because I hear this so much, "I live a good life, I'm a good person, I don't need any help, especially from God! Hum..., God feels a little different about this. The word of God tells us that all have sinned and come short of the glory of God; today is the day of Salvation, and the only way to heaven is through Jesus by being "Born Again".

We need to be immersed daily in the Holy Spirit, allowing the water of the Spirit to cleanse us from the dirt of the world that gets on us. Being washed by the Spirit of the Lord gives us a new outlook on life, and a peace that this world cannot offer.

We need the Lord; He doesn't need us. Jesus Loves us and He died and rose again on the 3rd day, just for you and me. He desires to fill us with his love and cleanse us so we can have eternal life. Heaven is only a breath away. When we allow God to fill us with his love and cleanse us through the Holy Spirit, fear will be replaced with peace - the peace that passes all understanding and only comes from Jesus.

Will you allow the Holy Spirit to renew your life today?

Will she *immerse* and *soak* in the presence of Almighty God?

She Will!

Lord, submerge us in your love and let us take a moment today to soak in your loving kindness that is greater than life itself. Teach us to be strong and courageous to fight the enemy that desires to take us out. Help us Lord to fall in love with you today, lay at your feet and bask in your love, wash me today, cleanse me within by your Holy Spirit and grant me the peace that no man can offer.

Bev

Your Thoughts....

Will She Anchor Deep?

_____
_____
_____
_____
_____
_____
_____
_____
_____
_____
_____
_____
_____
_____
_____
_____
_____

.... shewill!!!

Week 10

2 Chronicles 5:14 KJV

"So that the priests could not stand to minister by reason of the cloud: for the glory of the LORD had filled the house of God."

To sit in the sweet presence of the Lord, what a glorious place to be. I have been to many churches and gatherings where the presence of the Lord was with us. His sweet anointing upon us, the Holy Spirit offering everything our hearts need, if only we will receive it. When we become vulnerable as a body of Christ and as individuals, that's where the Lord meets us.

We leave church or a conference or a time of gathering with other believers, and we are so full from our experience! However, when we get home, the fight becomes real to keep that fullness.

Today, let me encourage you to cry out to Abba Father, Jehovah Jireh, the God that provides.

Ask Him for His sweet anointing. Ask His Holy Spirit to be with you each moment of the day.

Worship Him in the shower as you get ready for your day and as you drive. Honor Him, and He will honor you right back. He will be with you! Just like the priests in the temple, you'll come to a place where the glory of the Lord will fill the house of God (your temple which is your body) to a point that you will simply only need to be still and soak Him in.

Will She walk in His Holy Presence every step?

She Will!

Lord, we pray today for your glory to be with us, in us, through us, around us and about us. We invite Your Holy Spirit to have Your way in us. Our bodies are Your temple, Your house, and we consecrate ourselves to You. We give You everything we are. Our mind, body, soul, spirit and will are yours. Come Holy Spirit and fill us with Your sweet anointing every moment of our day, in Jesus' name, Amen.

Sara

Your Thoughts....

Will She Anchor Deep?

_____

_____

_____

_____

_____

_____

_____

_____

_____

_____

_____

_____

_____

_____

_____

.... shewill!!!

Week 11

Psalm 42:1-2 NIV

"As the deer pants for streams of water, so my soul pants for you, my God. My soul thirsts for God, for the living God. When can I go and meet with God?"

Have you ever been very thirsty? Yet you were far from the source to get a drink?

This scripture reminds us to thirst for our God, we are to be thirsty because He is our living water. Spiritual thirst is a longing for the presence of God in our lives.

Our soul, our mind, and our emotions, the deepest part of our being should be thirsty for our God because He is the only thing that can truly satisfy.

Our thoughts should be on Jesus who is our living water. Our will should be the Lord's will, our emotions should rejoice as we drink in the presence of the Lord.

Emotions, overflowing with peace and joy.

Will She thirst for the Living God?

She Will!

Father, thank you for Jesus my living water. My soul is satisfied in You Lord. You salt our oats to make us thirsty. Then we come to You for a drink of refreshing water.

That water not only refreshes me, but it strengthens me for my day. Thank you, heavenly Father for Jesus.

In His name, Amen.

Joy

Your Thoughts….

Will She Anchor Deep?

_____

_____

_____

_____

_____

_____

_____

_____

_____

_____

_____

_____

_____

_____

_____

_____

.... shewill!!!

Week 12

John 15:4 AMPC

"Dwell in Me, and I will dwell in you. [Live in Me, and I will live in you.] Just as no branch can bear fruit of itself without abiding in (being vitally united to) the vine, neither can you bear fruit unless you abide in Me."

The people that lived in John's Day would have been very familiar with the growing of grapes on the vine, and the various products made from them. Although my family had grapevines across the back of our garden one summer, I really don't know much about the process. I do know that if you break off part of the plant, you interrupt the flow of nutrients, and therefore halt the production of good fruit. If John was speaking to us today, I wonder if perhaps he would use a different analogy that might be more familiar to us.

Think of all the electronic devices that surround us today – Smartphones, computers, television sets, and more. These are all designed to bring us information, and are essential to many aspects of our daily lives, but how effective would they be if they were never plugged into an electrical source? Earlier today, a tractor trailer hit a power transformer near my house. All electricity stopped until the power company could reroute us to another source. Although a minor inconvenience, if the outage had lasted a longer period of time, it would have caused greater and greater distress, damage and decay.

What is your source of power, direction, and purpose? Does it originate with abiding in Jesus, learning on Him through prayer, teaching and preaching from the Word of God, and fellowship with other Christ-followers? Or does it come from the worldly influences in our lives?

In the Greek, the word used here for abide suggests remaining united with him, one with him in heart, mind, and will. Are you "vitally united to" Jesus as your source all throughout your day, in every area of your life?

Will She live her life united to Jesus as a deep anchor?

She Will!

Lord Jesus, please help me look to you daily as the source, guide, and director of my life. Help me to bear good fruit that reflects a desire to walk in the same manner as Jesus walked (1 John 2:6). Dwell in me so that when others see me, they see You. Amen.

Laura Anne

Zodhiates, S., Baker, W., & Hadjiantoniou, G. (Eds.) (1992). The Complete Word Study Dictionary: New Testament. AMG Publisher.

Your Thoughts….

Will She Anchor Deep?

_____

_____

_____

_____

_____

_____

_____

_____

_____

_____

_____

_____

_____

_____

_____

_____

.... *shewill!!!*

Week 13

Isaiah 43:2 NIV

"When you pass through the waters, I will be with you; and when you pass through the rivers, they will not sweep over you."

My Mother passed along her fear of water to me. Although I have struggled with that fear, I did learn to swim. "Perfect love casts out all fear" (1 John 4:18). I am not a strong swimmer though.

Many times, when I get in deep waters or can't see the bottom, I panic. I must calm myself and allow my swimming skills to take over.

In life we pass through troubled waters. We become overwhelmed with life's problems. Fear rises up and wants to take hold, wants to drown us in worry, doubt, and disappointment. Where there is fear there is not peace. The Bible tells us that Jesus came to give us peace, not as the world gives, but supernatural peace that surpasses understanding. Jesus says do not let our hearts be troubled and do not be afraid. (John 14:27) In 2 Timothy 1:7 it says that God has not given us a spirit of fear, but of power, love, and a sound mind.

Knowing God's promises keeps us from being swept over by the waves; surges of life that come swiftly.

Where is our anchor? Is our anchor set deep to steady us? Is the Word hidden in our hearts?

Do we go to the Word?

Life is difficult sometimes…divorce, marriage, illness, financial problems, worldly happenings. All can overwhelm us without a strong anchor in the Lord and His Word.

God's strength and promises are in The Word and allow us to swim in the deep waters. Where do you have your anchor? Who or what is your anchor in?

Will She anchor deep?

Yes, She Will!

Father, life is tough sometimes. Thank you that your Word promises us that you will walk through this life with us. When we falter Lord, we know you as our anchor, are there to steady us and You are a deep anchor that holds us steady.

Jo Ann

Your Thoughts....

Will She Anchor Deep?

_____
_____
_____
_____
_____
_____
_____
_____
_____
_____
_____
_____
_____
_____
_____
_____
_____
_____

.... *shewill!!!*

Week 14

Isaiah 12:3 NLT

"With joy you will drink deeply from the fountain of salvation!"

Nothing is more refreshing than cold water right out of the water hose after a day in the scorching heat dragging brush, clearing land, and throwing rocks. To turn on the faucet and watch the water flow, knowing there is no end until I turn it off, is a gratifying feeling especially after a hard day at work. I not only drink deeply, but I also wash my hands and splash my face. It is refreshing. I am thankful. I turn to this source of freshwater time after time throughout the day to quench my thirst. I do the hard work and then I drink and then I rejoice. My joy is found in the fact that I can constantly return for a drink; minute by minute, hour by hour, day by day and it is without end and readily available to me.

This is such a great word picture for us as we study the above scripture. Another translation says to "draw from the well". Both, drink, and draw are active verbs showing us we must do in order to get. The fountain of salvation is a gift that has been given to us, but we need to draw from it, drink deeply, daily.

Draw from the well that has no ending; ever flowing, always available and never runs dry. A well that never runs dry is good news, Beloved! There is not a limit as to how many times you can return to pull from the deep source of life-giving water. This is the reason for such joy!

A source of deliverance is another way of saying fountain of salvation. An inexhaustible source where we can go daily to be saved in the midst of our troubles. Where does our source of deliverance come from? Psalm 34:17 The righteous cry out, and the LORD hears them; he delivers them from all their troubles.

Our deep well is found only in the Lord. He is the well that has no end.

No matter what is going on in your life the saving grace of Christ is sufficient for you. (2 Cor 12:9) Whether you are in a battle of scorching heat, clearing, pruning the land God has given you, or throwing off those heavy emotional rocks, the deep well is there with refreshing, cleansing, healing, purifying water that will satisfy your thirst and bring joy to your soul.

Will She return to the well and drink deeply daily?

She Will!

Father, thank you for being a well so deep and so wide that provides for my every need. May I understand the importance of returning to you daily and allowing your Holy Spirit to flow through me. With joy I say thank you for your saving grace that meets me wherever I am. In Jesus name, Amen.

Shelsea

Your Thoughts….

Will She Anchor Deep?

_____
_____
_____
_____
_____
_____
_____
_____
_____
_____
_____
_____
_____
_____
_____
_____
_____
_____

.... shewill!!!

Week 15

Isaiah 44:3 NIV

"For I will pour water on the thirsty land, and streams on the dry ground; I will pour out my Spirit on your offspring, and my blessing on your descendants."

Do you ever feel as if you are in a drought? Whether it be spiritual, emotional, and/ or physical? Do you feel as if you are dried up, thirsty, and wrung out? Are you on the brink of exhaustion?

God is our restoration. (1 Peter 5:10) God sees us. He sees the bruises and bumps that life leaves on us. He sees us drying out. Fortunately for us, God doesn't leave us in our state of thirst. He finds us and pours out His Spirit.

He refreshes us by quenching our thirst. By blessing us with his Spirit, our souls begin to become refreshed and re-energized. By doing this, God is drawing near to us. His Spirit stirs our souls. He wants to refill you with His love, joy, peace, and blessings. God wants to pour Himself out to us because he loves us. (Acts 2:17) He desires an intimate relationship. When we enter into that relationship with Him, He will become our living water, and we will never thirst again.

God pours himself out in pursuance of you. He sees you and wants to refresh and bless you.

Will She allow her thirst to be quenched?

Yes, She Will!

Dear Jesus,

I thank you for being a God that pursues me. Thank you for choosing me. Thank you for finding me valuable enough to be recognized by you. Please refresh and renew my spirit. Quench my thirst. Thank you for pouring out your Spirit. Please continue doing so. Amen.

Savanna

Your Thoughts....

Will She Anchor Deep?

_____
_____
_____
_____
_____
_____
_____
_____
_____
_____
_____
_____
_____
_____
_____
_____
_____
_____

.... shewill!!!

Week 16

Isaiah 33:6 NIV

"He will be the sure foundation for your times, a rich store of salvation and wisdom and knowledge; the fear of the Lord is the key to this treasure."

We live in uncertain times; at every turn we see the evidence of the last days coming to fruition right in front of us. It is during these last days that we must trust in God to take care of us; we must anchor ourselves in Him alone.

More than ever, we see people searching for answers in all the wrong places and we must stay the course. God is the same yesterday, today, and forever.

We can trust that He is in total control and has everything we need to make it through. He is rich with salvation, wisdom, and knowledge. There is no need to look anywhere else.

Matthew 6:33

"But seek first his kingdom and his righteousness, and all these things will be given to you as well."

When we anchor ourselves to truth, we will have the peace that comes with it.

Let's look at it like this-- as we drive along life's highway, we can become distracted by the flashing lights, detours, and other drivers. If we allow ourselves to be distracted that can lead to our harm. If we want to live victorious, we must keep our focus on the road ahead. That means trusting in God and His foundation. When we are anchored deep in Christ, we don't have to be afraid, The Lord will see us through, we will arrive to our eternal destination safe and sound.

Isaiah 41:10

"Fear not, for I am with you; Be not dismayed, for I am your God. I will strengthen you."

Will you keep your eyes on Christ?

Will She Anchor Deep?

She Will!

Dear Lord, help me to anchor deep in you and the foundation of your word today. Lead me with your wisdom and knowledge. Give me your peace when the things of this world frighten me. I will walk closely with you, keeping my eyes on you. I will trust in your foundation and keep my eyes fixed on you to avoid the distraction the enemy puts in my path. I will put my faith in you,

I will anchor deep!

In Jesus' Name

Victoria

Your Thoughts....

Will She Anchor Deep?

_____

_____

_____

_____

_____

_____

_____

_____

_____

_____

_____

_____

_____

_____

_____

_____

.... _shewill!!!_

Week 17

Exodus 40:34 NIV

"Then the cloud covered the tent of meeting, and the glory of the LORD filled the tabernacle."

After fleeing Egypt and disobeying God's instruction to go into the Promised Land, God disciplined the Israelites with 40 years of wandering in the wilderness. But, like a good Father, God did not abandon His children during their consequence. He was right there with them, continuing to love, direct, and grow them through that season of discipline.

It was during that time that God instructed Moses to build the tabernacle. The tabernacle was a portable tent-like structure in which God said He would dwell. Every time they changed locations, the Israelites disassembled the tabernacle and took it with them. When they found their next stopping place, they'd reassemble the tabernacle and resume making their sacrifices to God.

Exodus 40 describes Moses setting up the tabernacle for the first time. Once everything was in its proper place, "the glory of the LORD filled the tabernacle." God's majesty and splendor saturated the inner room of the tabernacle, and there He would stay until it was time to move again.

To "tabernacle" means to dwell. When we accept Jesus as our Lord and Savior, Ephesians says Christ dwells in our hearts through faith. Similarly, 1 Corinthians says the believer's body is God's temple (or tabernacle) in which God's Spirit dwells. In other words, since the resurrection of Christ, God hasn't needed a tabernacle or temple to dwell in; His glory fills our bodies!

What does it feel like to be filled with the Spirit?

What difference does it make to know that God's glory saturates our bodies?

Every moment we live is an opportunity to soak in God's presence. He is closer than our own skin! And He gives us the choice to consciously meditate on that fact, letting it stir us to praise, or to largely ignore that fact, preventing it from making any difference in our lives.

Will She soak in God's presence within her?

She Will!

Father, it is a beautiful mystery how You, the Lord of Lords, and King of Kings, somehow dwells within us by faith. Thank You for desiring to be that close to us! Help us be awed by Your nearness. May we marvel at Your presence regularly. Help us to be constantly aware of Your Spirit dwelling within us and let us live in ways that honor Your presence. Amen!

Kelly

Your Thoughts....

Will She Anchor Deep?

_____
_____
_____
_____
_____
_____
_____
_____
_____
_____
_____
_____
_____
_____
_____
_____
_____
_____
_____

.... shewill!!!

Week 18

Hebrews 6:7 -NLT

"When the ground soaks up the falling rain and bears a good crop for the farmer, it has God's blessing."

God is telling us to soak in his Word, his truths and we shall see blessings. "Soak in the falling rain…" He continues to say in verse 8, but if a field bears thorns and thistles, it is useless. The farmer will soon condemn that field and burn it.

This passage reminds me of being a child. I was saved and baptized. Fast forward about 30 years, and I start questioning if I'm really saved? Is that all? How can I just say a few words and be dunked under water and be done? - God answered, because you're not done. I don't want to be that farmer, that evil one who is tossed away. I want all of God's truth I can receive and share. As Christians we need to not leave a new Christian on a rock to figure it out on their own.

We need to teach them and grow them.

Will She soak with the Lord?

She Will!

Lord, I ask that today be a day that I just soak you in more and more. And from this day forward God I ask that you help guide me, you help me with my lack of patience, and you bring me other believers to surround me through my journey of getting to know you better. In Jesus name, Amen.

Dawn

Your Thoughts….

Will She Anchor Deep?

_____

_____

_____

_____

_____

_____

_____

_____

_____

_____

_____

_____

_____

_____

_____

_____

_____

_____

_____

.... shewill!!!

Week 19

John 4:14 NIV

". but whoever drinks the water I give them will never thirst. Indeed, the water I give them will become in them a spring of water welling up to eternal life."

The woman at the well, we think we know so much about her, but much of what we think we know isn't even in the story. We are told she went to the well late to avoid other women and ridicule. That's possible. It's also possible that wild living caused the Samaritan woman to sleep in. Maybe her whole life drug along off kilter, off schedule, and more difficult than it needed to be. We forget; women could not seek divorce in that day. At least five different men had taken her, used her, then rejected her. We do not know the details of her sin because Jesus focused on her needs rather than her failures. She needed water and came with a jug to get it.

The location likely inspired her question, "Are you greater than Jacob, John 4:12?" Remember, this was not just any well. It was Jacob's Well, John 4:5-6. Even then, it was a sacred site.

Once, Jacob had been there. The patriarch had been given promises. Everyone had a promise, the Messiah would come from Jacob, Numbers 24:17.

Soon, the one whose thirst was prophesied in Psalm 22:15, would cry out in thirst from the cross, John 19:28. As a weary traveler, Jesus sat beside a spiritually thirsty outcast at Jacob's Well and offered living water, John 4:10. In a culture desperate for water, living water was a familiar concept. It was not stagnant or salty. Moving and active like rain or a flowing spring, living water brought life.

Others could water flocks. They could receive promises and provide water for a day. Jesus guaranteed more than an end to their dryness. Jesus vowed a river that welled up bringing eternal life. Only the Messiah could pledge something like that. Jesus did not claim to be that water. He promised to give it. That water is the Holy Spirit, John 7:37–39. It would be poured out like water, Acts 10:44–45.

There is so much we do not know about the Samaritan woman. We do know she was looking for the Messiah and He made Himself known to her. We know that she came empty and thirsty and left so full she left her jug behind. We know the rivers flowing out of her called her community to Christ. We know that no one who trusts in Him will ever go thirsty, John 6:35.

And we know the answer to her question. Is Jesus greater than Jacob? The answer is a resounding yes! Acts 4:12, Philippians 2:9!

Will She become like a spring of water welling up with new life?

She Will!

Jesus, we thank you that because of you we can be saved, and our thirst can be quenched. Let your Holy Spirit fill us to overflowing. Let the life flowing from us draw others to you. Enable us to yield to the Spirit's flow.

Julie

Your Thoughts….

Will She Anchor Deep?

_____

_____

_____

_____

_____

_____

_____

_____

_____

_____

_____

_____

_____

_____

_____

.... *shewill!!!*

Week 20

1 John 1:9 NKJV

"If we confess our sins, He is faithful and just to forgive us our sins and to cleanse us from all unrighteousness."

This verse is one of at least seven IF/THEN statements made by John in this chapter. An IF/THEN statement leads us to believe that IF we are obedient in the request made THEN there is a reward. Obviously, as a believer we have received the greatest reward of all--eternal salvation!

So, one might ask, "Why then do we need to continue to ask for forgiveness of our sins if Jesus forgave us upon receiving Him as our Lord and Savior?" ...the answer is simple. Sin creates a barrier. Think of it this way; when you have an argument with a loved one, you may think to yourself, "They know that I love them so there is no reason to apologize." Is this true? Yes and no... Yes, they should know that regardless of the argument you love them and most likely they love you still. But the disagreement between you, if not resolved and forgiven, will always be there...like a stone building a wall. Eventually the wall is too high to see over, and you have lost your relationship with that person.

Confessing our sin and asking for forgiveness removes our sin's impact on our relationship with God. Most assuredly the sin was on our part, and yes, He will continue to love us, but without confession and forgiveness we give Satan a foothold to build a wall between us and God.

Are you building a wall today with unconfessed sin?

Will She be obedient to confess her sins?

She Will!

Jesus, it is only through you that we are made right, righteous, before God. And it's in you that forgiveness is available...because of what you did at Calvary. Your sacrifice was great, so our willingness to confess our sins often is the least we could offer you. I thank you that you are faithful and just to forgive us each time we come to you with an obedient and humble heart. It's in your precious name we pray. Amen.

Liz

Your Thoughts....

Will She Anchor Deep?

_____

_____

_____

_____

_____

_____

_____

_____

_____

_____

_____

_____

_____

_____

_____

_____

_____

.... shewill!!!

Week 21

2 Samuel 22:17 NIV

"He reached down from on high and took hold of me; he drew me out of deep waters."

I looked up through the muddy waters and caught a glimpse of my cousin trying to fight the water and grasp my hand. I had seen my younger cousin slip into a sinkhole and was trying to save him, but soon realized I too was going down. My older cousin by 9 months, Steve, happened to see me and was making a frantic grab to save me. The waters were too swift and deep for him too. I succumbed to the muddy waters surrounding me and the warm peace that began enveloping my being. Before I drifted into oblivion and death, I was being yanked back up into the sunlight. My uncle saw the top of Steve's head as he submerged and grabbed him.

Much to his surprise he also had me holding Steve's hand and I holding my younger cousin's hand.

Have you ever felt like you were drowning? Sometimes it's not waters that threaten to suck out our life, but circumstances. Death, divorce, bankruptcy, loss of a job, failures, the list is endless, and we've all been there.

In the above verse, the Psalmist David is extolling the praises of God because he snatched him from deep waters.

He was chased un-mercifully by Saul, his enemy, and could see death swirling around him.

We all have an enemy who chases us and desires to destroy us.

Jesus told the loud mouthed, boisterous Peter, "Satan has desired to sift each of you as wheat."

Meaning, he wants to shake you so badly, you lose hope and drown.

Earlier, when Peter saw Jesus walking on the water, he wanted to join him. Soon though, the waves began washing up around his legs and the winds began to knock him around and down he went.

Jesus looked down with compassion and drew him out of the waters. Not because he deserved it. Not because he was perfect. No, he knew he needed a savior, and that savior loved him enough to pull him from the deep waters.

Are you sinking in despair due to life's circumstances?

Will She be saved and lifted out of the deep waters?

She Will!

Jesus, we cry out just like the Psalmist David and boisterous Peter. Save us! We're sinking and about to lose hope. We extend our hands to you, take hold Lord, and draw us from these deep waters. Amen.

Thresa

Your Thoughts….

Will She Anchor Deep?

_____

_____

_____

_____

_____

_____

_____

_____

_____

_____

_____

_____

_____

_____

_____

_____

.... _shewill!!!_

Week 22

Psalm 27:4

"One thing have I asked from the LORD, that I shall seek:
That I may dwell in the house of the LORD all the days of my
life,
To behold the beauty of the LORD
And to meditate in His temple."

I love what John Wesley said about this scripture: Dwell. - Have opportunity of constant attendance upon God. To behold - That there I may delight myself, in the contemplation of thy amiable and glorious majesty, and of thy infinite wisdom, holiness, justice, truth, and mercy.

When we are falling in love and thinking this is the one, I have longed for, to spend the rest of my life with. We can't seem to get enough of them. We stay up late and get up early to do everything possible just to be with the one we love. We desire to dwell in their presence. There is nothing we wouldn't do for this man. He feels the same way he'd pull the moon from the sky if that's what she wanted. The longing to be in each other's arms of love and safety.

This is how God wants us to long for him. To long, to dwell in his presence, to seek after him. We are in a fast-paced world, and we want everything done quick and now! Microwave everything, just so you can eat faster and move on to something else. Work keeps us all so very busy and kids playing 5 different sports going 5 different directions, who has time to dwell? Who has time to soak in our hot tubs and spas, for that matter? Hum.

Well God is still in the loving, soaking and dwelling business, aren't we glad to hear that? We have gotten so wrapped up in our day to day, we have forgotten to dwell and soak, not only as a family but as a child of God.

Doesn't it put the biggest smile on your face and in your heart when one of your kids or your spouse comes up to you and gives you a hug and a kiss just because? or they just want to hang out with you.

God feels that way too. He wants us to desire to dwell in his presence and soak in the beauty of his love.

In Psalms 27, King David is praising God with words of adoration: God is still a God that loves and longs to hear the praises from his people.

Are you one of God's people? Are you so in love with the one that gave everything for you, so you could have the hope of eternal life?

Are you singing praises to God and soaking in the goodness of his grace and mercy? Do you desire to dwell in the house of the Lord in his presence? Better is one day in the presence of the Lord than a thousand elsewhere.

Who do you desire to worship?

Will She dwell in the presence of the Almighty?

She Will!

God, forgive me for being so busy in my life that I have not taken time to dwell in your presence. Lord, I want to dwell in your house and soak in the beauty of your grace and mercy all the days of my life. Help me to desire and delight in your holiness and to walk in your path and not my own. In Jesus name, Amen.

Bev

Your Thoughts....

Will She Anchor Deep?

_____

_____

_____

_____

_____

_____

_____

_____

_____

_____

_____

_____

_____

_____

_____

.... shewill!!!

Week 23

John 4:10 NLT

Jesus replied, "If you only knew the gift God has for you and who you are speaking to, you would ask me, and I would give you living water."

This is Jesus's reply to the Samaritan woman at the well. She was shocked that a Jew would speak to her and offer her living water. A woman who had five husbands and was living with a man who was not her husband at the time of the encounter. Jesus's disciples were shocked at his speaking to the woman, yet they did not have the courage to question Him. Jesus saw her so worthy to offer her living water and a personal encounter with Him. As she became aware of who she was speaking, the actual Messiah, she ran to tell everyone. Jesus told her there would be a time where we could worship from anywhere. Where true worshippers will worship in spirit and in truth. That is for us today, and the living water offered so long ago to the Samaritan woman is offered to you and me right now. If only we knew the gift God has for us, and who we are speaking to! We would ask Him, and He would give us living water.

God blessed me by allowing me to minister to women in a prison. Right there amongst the cells,

I worshiped with women from all walks of life. They were thirsty. As we cried out to Jesus, He came for us right there. Are you thirsty today? Do you need Him? He says to ask for His living waters, and He will give it to you. Today, no matter what you've done or where you are, Jesus is right there, hands outreached to you saying, "Ask me child." Ask Him today for His living water, and believe with all your heart that He will give you what You ask for as it aligns with His word.

Oh, beloved sister, it's simply who He is.

Will She immerse herself in His living waters?

She Will!

Father, we come to You today, and we ask for Your living water. We can hardly fathom the gift God has for us, yet we desire it so greatly. We invite You in and ask for Your living water. Fill us today and lead us on Your paths of righteousness. Help us to keep our eyes wholly fixed upon You on this day, in Jesus Name, Amen.

Sara

Your Thoughts….

Will She Anchor Deep?

_____

_____

_____

_____

_____

_____

_____

_____

_____

_____

_____

_____

_____

_____

.... shewill!!!

Week 24

Revelation 22:17

"The Spirit and the bride say, "Come!" And let him who hears say "Come!" And let him who thirsts come. Whoever desires, let him take the water of life freely."

The Spirit of God; the Holy Spirit and the bride; the Church says, "Come!" This is an invitation without an RSVP. There is not an expiration date. If you have ears to hear, then tell everyone to come!

If you thirst for God, you are invited to take of the water of life freely. The Lord has given us an invitation to come to Him.

Whoever means, anyone everyone that is if you are thirsty for the Lord. If you hear the truth of the gospel (Good news) of Jesus Christ and you respond by coming to Him, you will be saved, free of any guilt or shame, and your thirst will be quenched.

Take freely without payment the gift of life-giving water.

Will She take the water of life?

She Will!

Father God, thank you for the life of Jesus. Thank you that as we come with a thirsty heart and a willing mind to receive all that He has provided for us, we are saved and have a new life. We are loved unconditionally. Thank you for loving me. In Jesus name, Amen.

Joy

Your Thoughts….

Will She Anchor Deep?

_____

_____

_____

_____

_____

_____

_____

_____

_____

_____

_____

_____

_____

_____

.... shewill!!!

Week 25

Hebrews 10:22 NIV

"Let us draw near to God with a sincere heart and with the full assurance that faith brings, having our hearts sprinkled to cleanse us from a guilty conscience and having our bodies washed with pure water."

What does it mean to cleanse? According to the Oxford English dictionary, cleanse is defined as to make thoroughly clean, or to cure. In 1 John 1:9 NISB, it says, "If we confess our sins, He is faithful and righteous to forgive us our sins and to cleanse us from all unrighteousness." When we first come to Jesus, confess our belief that Jesus Christ is Lord, and are saved (Romans 10:9), we are freed from the burden of shame.

How does that help us to have the full assurance that faith brings? Let me tell you a story. I was barely sixteen years old when my boyfriend attempted to teach me to drive his stick-shift car. I remember cresting the top of the hill on the way back to my house, jubilant with the feeling that I just might be getting the hang of it, when blue lights and sirens appeared behind me. The state trooper insisted that I get out of the car, and that my boyfriend remain seated. He reached in, grabbed the keys from the ignition and threw them on the roof of the car. I was terrified! He asked if he knew how fast I was going, and I remember thinking that I was just glad that I figured out where fourth gear was. Apparently, I was very familiar with the gas pedal. The citation was sizable. Now, I had to go home, and tell my dad.

My boyfriend drove us back to my house; I was shaking from adrenaline. As I hesitantly approached the door, I had full assurance that I would be received, and that we would work

through the situation.

While it may seem a rather trivial example, fear, shame, and guilt can keep us from approaching our Heavenly Father.

When I approached my heavenly Father, with gut-wrenching sobs, pouring out myself in a puddle on the floor, confessing, repenting, praying, I had the full assurance that God would receive me, that He still loved me unconditionally. Yes, my choices still had consequences, and there would certainly be challenges ahead as a result, but I didn't allow my shame to separate me from God. Through it all, I was never alone; My God anchored me.

When she feels like she is drowning in shame, Will She anchor deep?

She Will!

Lord, please help us study the Bible, the Word of God, so that we can know your character.

That will help us to trust your love for us is greater than our shame. We cannot trust someone that we don't know. Thank you, Lord, for making a way for us to be reconciled to you through the blood of Jesus Christ, just as if we hadn't sinned. Amen.

Laura Anne

Stevenson, A., Waite, M. (Eds.) (2011). Concise Oxford English Dictionary. Oxford University Press.

Your Thoughts….

Will She Anchor Deep?

_____

_____

_____

_____

_____

_____

_____

_____

_____

_____

_____

_____

_____

_____

.... shewill!!!

Week 26

James 4:8 NLT

"Come close to God and God will come close to you. Wash your hands, you sinner; purify your hearts for your loyalty is divided between God and the world."

Come Close.

Have you ever expected company at your house, and you are excited? Someone you are anxious to see? When our children and grandchildren come to see us, I am usually in the kitchen cooking all their favorites. As they pull up in the driveway, I quickly wash my hands and go out to greet them. I can't wait for them to get out of their cars, so the grandkids can start running toward me for their hugs. We run toward each other because of love.

Have you ever run toward God? His hands are outstretched waiting for us so he can wrap us in his strong arms. His love is overwhelming. God is love. (1 John 4:16) James 4:8 promises us that if we draw near to God, He will draw near to us.

When we approach Him are we going toward God with a purified heart? Are we excited to run to Lord? Are our sins confessed? Is our mind cleared from worldly clutter?

Running toward God, who is running to us. Can you imagine? God runs to us, so we run to Him.

Then together we run with endurance this life race which is our purpose.

Will She dig deep in the Word?

Will She run toward God?

Yes, She Will, and He will anchor her deep and steady!

Father, I am here drawing close to you. Your word promises me that if I do that, you will come close to me. I need you to be close, Lord. I do not want anything to keep me separated from you.

Forgive me for trying to live in both worlds. Please purify my heart and bring anything to my mind that I need to repent of. I want to run to you in full surrender. Thank you for running to me too!

In Jesus name, Amen.

Jo Ann

Your Thoughts....

Will She Anchor Deep?

_____

_____

_____

_____

_____

_____

_____

_____

_____

_____

_____

_____

_____

_____

.... shewill!!!

Week 27

Revelation 21:6 NASB

"Then He said to me, "It is done. I am the Alpha and the Omega, the beginning, and the end. I will give to the one who thirsts from the spring of the water of life without cost."

Who is speaking here? I AM!

We are introduced to I AM in the book of Exodus 3:14 when Moses asks God who shall I say has sent me? The Lord responds with I AM WHO I AM. In Revelation he says I Am and then adds to it by saying the Alpha and the Omega, the beginning, and the end. In the book of John, he tells us in the beginning was the Word, and the Word was with God, and the Word was God.

He goes on to say that the Word became flesh and dwelt among us. Who dwelt among us?

Jesus!

We see Jesus in the beginning, and we will see him face to face when He returns for his Bride.

How glorious that day will be! Until then, He is offering us the spring of life at absolutely no cost.

We can live a life of fullness in the here and now if we choose, if we thirst. Jesus said that he came to earth to give us life, that his purpose was to give us a fullness and richness on this side

of heaven. (John 10:10) After Jesus ascended, He sent us His Holy Spirit. (Acts 2) When we drink from this spring of life, we receive more than we can ask or imagine. (Eph 3:20)

The Lord paints me beautiful pictures when I am around water. He speaks His truths to me through nature. Here is one of those times:

As I traversed through a creek that was fed by a natural spring, I was amazed at how much pure spring water was coming from such a small hole. The spring water was continually flowing from the belly of the earth through an opening no larger than the size of a quarter. The more it flowed, the more water that filled the creek. Without this natural spring the creek would dry up.

This creek feeds the adjoining river. Without this creek, the river would die. The river was being sustained by the source of the natural spring.

As I was sitting out in the middle of this creek, I felt the Lord impress upon my heart the comparison of this river that relied on the spring as its source to that of my heart that relies on the continual flow of the Holy Spirit; spring of the water of life. I noticed upriver that there was a block in the flow of water. Rocks and debris were washed into the stream from a previous storm.

Without removal of these blockades, the river will dry up.

This is true for all of us. Our spirits are connected to the Spirit of God but can be subject to hinderance when the storms of life come through and we haven't done the hard and holy work of removing the debris. Our rivers can die, our spirits can be quenched. The spring of life is there but we must move out, work through the things we have hidden deep inside; unforgiveness, emotional trauma, wounds, fears, failures. When we are brave and address these issues of life head on, the Spirit wells up within us and out of our bellies shall flow rivers of living water. (John 7:38)

Will She be brave and remove life's debris?

Will She thirst for the springs of life?

She Will!

Heavenly Father, please bring to my attention the debris that is in the way of your Holy Spirit from freely flowing in my life.

Shelsea

Your Thoughts….

Will She Anchor Deep?

_____
_____
_____
_____
_____
_____
_____
_____
_____
_____
_____
_____
_____
_____
_____

…. *shewill!!!*

Week 28

Psalm 51:10 NIV

"Create in me a clean heart, O God, and renew a right spirit within me."

As the result of the fall of humanity, sin entered the world. Sin separates us from God.

However, through the grace, mercy, and redemption of Jesus Christ's death, we are given the ability to remain close to the Lord. To be able to do this fully, we must believe that God is the Lord of this world. We must also confess and repent of our sins.

When we do this, God can now come in and refresh and renew our spirits. He can make our spirits right again. Having a right spirit means that your spirit aligns with the Holy Spirit. This allows for God's Spirit to reside inside of you. The Holy Spirit then can really work in you. The Holy Spirit will reveal truths to you. He will then move and work through you.

When you have a right spirit, you are able to be in tune with the ways of the Holy Spirit.

You can see where God is working and where you are supposed to fit in with that.

So, ladies, let us get a refresher for our spirits! Let's become involved with the work of God!

Will She ask God to renew her heart and soul?

Oh, yes, She Will!

Dear Heavenly Father,

Thank you for your forgiveness and mercy. Thank you for healing my heart and my soul.

Refresh me. Please draw your Spirit near to mine. Renew me so that I may be able to accomplish what you call me to. Include me in your mission!

Lots of love! Amen.

Savanna

Your Thoughts....

Will She Anchor Deep?

_____

_____

_____

_____

_____

_____

_____

_____

_____

_____

_____

_____

_____

_____

_____

_____

.... shewill!!!

Week 29

Proverbs 20:5 MSG

"Knowing what is right is like deep water in the heart; a wise person draws from the well within."

Which way should I go, which is the best thing for me? Is it time for a career change, should I go back to school, Is it time to sell our house, should I marry him?

Questions like that and many others will arise in our lives, if we want to make the right decisions, we must seek the council of The Holy Spirit. He will teach us all things!

John 14:25-27 "I'm telling you these things while I'm still living with you. The Friend, the Holy Spirit whom the Father will send at my request, will make everything plain to you. He will remind you of all the things I have told you. I'm leaving you well and whole. That's my parting gift to you. Peace. I don't leave you the way you're used to being left—feeling abandoned, bereft. So don't be upset.

Don't be distraught.

My youngest son is quiet and a little more reserved. When he was in school, he faced bullies from time to time because of it. I remember back when he was in the 8th grade, he was being bullied at the first of the year. The Lord spoke to my heart and said pull him out of public school and home school him for the year. I knew it had to be God because I had never been called to that before, even with his 3 older brothers. I was intimidated but I knew The Lord had a plan and would not leave us, so facing our fears we jumped into the deep end!

Talk about diving in, we went headfirst into Classical Conversations as our curriculum! It's a big jump from where we were to learning Latin. That year was hard, but the harder it got, the more I would lean on The Lord. We came through to the other side and the Lord was glorified in so many ways! My son was stronger and more confident and went on to finish strong! I am forever grateful for that year, and all God taught us both. So, when you are faced with questions about where to go or what to do, dive deep in and pray for The Holy Spirit to show you what God has for you. It might be scary, but it will be the right way!

"In the Bible God speaks to us; in prayer we speak to God. Both are essential."

Billy Graham

Do you trust Him?

Will She dive deep?

She Will!

Dear Lord, teach me to trust you more, to learn that the deeper I dive into your word and listen to The Holy Spirit within me that I will accomplish all you have for me. Thank you for not leaving us as orphans, but stronger with the gift of The Holy Spirit! I love you and trust you God.

In Christ Name

Victoria

Your Thoughts....

Will She Anchor Deep?

_____

_____

_____

_____

_____

_____

_____

_____

_____

_____

_____

_____

_____

_____

_____

.... shewill!!!

Week 30

Proverbs 18:4 RSV

"The words of a man's mouth are deep waters; the fountain of wisdom is a gushing stream."

Many couplets in Proverbs reinforce one idea. (Fancy people call this "parallelism.")

Sometimes the author says the same thing in two different ways to emphasize one idea.

Sometimes he contrasts two ideas to make one point. And sometimes he states one idea and then expands that idea to make one point, which is what Solomon may be doing in this proverb.

The main idea is that the speech of a man is deep. This guy's words are profound, and, as a result, are a little hard to understand at first.

The second phrase clears up whether this is a good thing or not by likening the man to a "fountain of wisdom." The man's words being deep is actually a good thing and indicates his speech is wise.

Solomon adds that the man's wise words are not only deeply profound, but they are also like a gushing stream, never lacking or drying up, and flowing naturally.

The idea, then, is that we should aspire to have constantly and consistently wise, profound words to offer.

I don't know about you, but, left up to my own devices, my speech is more likely to contain superficial jokes/sarcasm (which, although DELIGHTFUL, don't always ooze pearls of "wisdom"). On the off chance that I say something serious, my words are usually Logical Opinions of How You Ought to Live Your Life According to How Kelly's Fallen Brain Works.

While I consider my speech wise, God doesn't always agree.

My "wisdom" is not what my friends, family, or terrible drivers need to hear at any given moment. They need the Lord's wisdom (and, perhaps, Driver's Ed.).

If I really want to honor God with my speech and help people walk in His ways, I need to speak His wisdom (which is really the only kind of wisdom there is, when we get down to it).

How do I consistently speak wisely? Jesus said, "The mouth speaks what the heart is full of." Gulp.

If we anchor deep in God's Word, His wisdom will come right off the pages of scripture and saturate our hearts and minds. Then, the Holy Spirit will bring those wise words to mind and to mouth when He wants us to say them.

There is a direct correlation between our scripture intake and our wisdom output.

Will She anchor deep in the Word to become a gushing stream of wisdom?

She Will!

Lord, we thank you for giving us easy access to Your wisdom in book form! We confess we take our Bibles for granted. Give us the desire and the power to read, study, and memorize scripture more! Help us anchor deeply in the Word every single day to prepare us for when the Spirit will prompt us to speak wisdom to others. May we do so humbly and biblically for Your glory. Amen!

Kelly

Your Thoughts….

Will She Anchor Deep?

_____
_____
_____
_____
_____
_____
_____
_____
_____
_____
_____
_____
_____
_____
_____
_____
_____
_____

.... *shewill!!!*

Week 31

Isaiah 58:11 NIV

"The Lord will guide you always; he will satisfy your needs in a sun-scorched land and will strengthen your frame. You will be like a well-watered garden, like a spring whose waters never fail."

When uncertainties rise, anchor deep in the word and the truths God tells you. Has anyone noticed the gas prices lately? Are you having to change plans because of this? That is just one example. Think back at any time in your life when uncertainties crept in. Did you go straight to the Father? Or did you keep it on your shoulders first? This verse right here tells us the Lord will guide you always; he will satisfy your needs.

During my first time being on leave from work due to medical issues, God provided. Yes, I lost my credit and my house I was renting. If I'm totally honest, God may have had a lesson in there for me also, maybe 2. But he never left my side, and all of my needs were met. My boys were able to help me sell products on the weekends at different market days to pay for my truck and phone. There have been many situations where God has shown up and satisfied our needs and guided our family. The devil will try to make you believe it is impossible. Our Lord as Savior is the one true King of making impossible possible.

Matthew 19:26

Jesus looked at them and said, "With man this is impossible, but with God all things are possible."

Will She immerse herself?

She Will!

Lord, I'm so grateful that you are there for us to guide us and satisfy our needs. I pray that as I immerse myself more into your word that you begin to speak through me. Use me and my testimonies to help others. In Jesus name, Amen.

Dawn

Your Thoughts….

Will She Anchor Deep?

_____

_____

_____

_____

_____

_____

_____

_____

_____

_____

_____

_____

_____

_____

.... shewill!!!

Week 32

Psalm 40:2 NIV

"He lifted me out of the slimy pit, out of the mud and mire; he set my feet on a rock and gave me a firm place to stand."

Pits are deadly places. Early on, scripture takes the time to warn us about their dangers, Exodus 21-33:34. Centuries later, Jeremiah must have clung to David's words as he waited for rescue, after King Zedekiah's pride landed the prophet in a pit, Jeremiah 38.

Who knows what, specifically, David had on his mind as he wrote the Psalm? It's possible David was remembering Joseph and how God worked a pit, born of jealousy, into good, Genesis 37:23-24, 50:20. Maybe, he was thinking of his own mighty men, Johnathan and Ahimaaz, who hid in a pit filled with darkness and silence as Absalom's forces sought their lives, 2 Samuel 17:17-21. Perhaps, David was reminiscing about another mighty man Benaiah, who willingly walked into a pit, as he stalked lions on a snowy day, 1 Chronicles 11:22. It is possible, if not probable, David was contemplating the pit into which his rebellious son Absalom's corpse was callously thrown, Samuel 18:14-15, 33.

Understand, a pit was more than a hole in the ground. The word can be synonymous with sin or suffering, with death, hell, and the grave. As a whole, Psalm 40 is a Psalm of lament, or weeping, which begins praising God for past rescue and returns to praise as the solution for enduring the current crisis. Of course, it is also a Messianic Psalm, looking forward to the One who could rescue Himself from the pit and provide a way out for all mankind. When Jesus conquered the pit, He lifted us, Zechariah 9:11, Jonah 2:6.

Before we are lifted, every one of us is trapped in muck and despair. The longer we are in the filth the deeper we sink and the harder it becomes to escape. Jesus not only raises us to liberty, He provides freedom with a firm foundation, where we can weather any storm, Matthew 7:24-27. Jesus is that rock, Deuteronomy 32:4. Whatever our pit, however we got there, we can be at peace. We can stand firmly on him.

Will She stand on the rock?

She Will!

Jesus, thank you for the pits you have saved me from. Thank you for the pits you have brought me through. Thank you that you were willing to conquer the pit. Thank you that because of you I can be clean and whole. Forgive me for any filthy thing I have embraced. Cause me to see the dangers and temptations in my path. Lift me out of any trenches and dark places in my life.

Embolden me to face suffering in my own life with a heart of praise. Enable me to live a life of holiness and purity for you and empower me to be a light for you.

Julie West

Your Thoughts….

Will She Anchor Deep?

_____

_____

_____

_____

_____

_____

_____

_____

_____

_____

_____

_____

_____

_____

_____

.... shewill!!!

Week 33

Psalm 23:2 NIV

"He makes me lie down in green pastures; he leads me beside quiet waters,"

When I was a child growing up in the suburbs of Houston, one of my favorite things was to lie in the lush San Augustine grass and visually explore the expanse of the heavens. I would lie there for hours, mentally forming animals and shapes from the clouds. To this day, I haven't found rest as complete as the times spent on the comfort of that vibrantly green blanket.

How do you find rest? Psalm 23 is all about rest; the rest we find when being led by the Spirit of God. He leads us to rest in green meadows; He leads us to rest by quiet streams. There's a good reason sleep apps include a trickling stream; it quiets our minds. One of my favorite scriptures is Psalm 42:1; As the deer pants for the water, so my soul longs after you Lord.

The deer knows to draw strength and refreshment from the quiet streams, so how much more should we draw our strength from the same source?

Psalm 23 starts with The Lord is my Shepherd, I shall not lack; If He is truly your Shepherd and Lord of your life, then you lack nothing! Rest in His provision today; stop striving to provide for yourself. Your efforts are fruitless; God provides with abundance! Peace in abundance; rest in abundance. All that you need today and more can be found in Him.

Where are you finding rest today?

Will She rest in the Lord?

She Will!

Heavenly Father, it is so much better your way! The rest we find in you is immeasurable...Thank you for shepherding us, leading us to the perfect rest in you. Amen.

Liz

Your Thoughts….

Will She Anchor Deep?

_____

_____

_____

_____

_____

_____

_____

_____

_____

_____

_____

_____

_____

.... shewill!!!

Week 34

Tim 4:12,13,15 MSG

"And don't let anyone put you down because you're young. Teach believers with your life: by word, by demeanor, by love, by faith, by integrity. Stay at your post reading Scripture, giving counsel, teaching.

Cultivate these things. Immerse yourself in them. The people will all see you mature right before their eyes!"

We've heard it said, "Your life is the only Bible some people read." Uh- ho, that is scary. Too many Christians don't even read the Bible, much less become a lens by which others can.

When Jesus called the disciples, He said, "Come follow me" (Mat 4:19; Mk 1:17) Paul said, "Follow me as I follow Christ" (I Cor 11:1, MEV). Are we a living epistle read by all men? (2 Cor 3:2-3).

When my granddaughter was three, she was my little shadow. I noticed that anytime she became frustrated she would growl. You know, that guttural sound similar to that of a dog. One day I questioned her, "Aubrielle, why are you growling?" Shortly after, we were getting in the car and as I opened the door something fell and wedged between the car seat and the side panel making it difficult to extricate. I growled. I stood up and laughed realizing the source of my granddaughter's new expression. Thankfully, I was also able to pass on good attributes.

Moses gave instructions to the children of Israel to obey the commands, decrees, and regulations that the Lord gave. If they did this, they would be prosperous and live long, healthy lives (Deut. 6:1-2). There is a benefit to studying and knowing the word. It is life. It is alive and active and as we read it, we become more alive. Too often we just glean from the corners, i.e.., scripture of the day someone else shared, or point and read method. Sadly, too often, once we are cleansed, we become stagnant with no life flowing out from us.

What is it you're needing today? Salvation? Hope? Comfort? It is there in the book that is more than ink and paper, it is living water. So, drink deeply and read. Become intimate with the words between the leather covers. Go deeper, immerse, and let the life gifting fountain begin to overflow from you to others.

Someone is in desperate need of a guide to show them the way to love, life and hope.

Will you immerse in the word of God?

Will She become a source of love, life and hope that others may glean from?

She Will!

Father, help us to not be so much about our own selfish desires. Rather, help us to be like sponges absorbing your word which is a life-giving fountain. Then, we can express this liquid love, life, and hope that the scriptures give.

Thresa

Your Thoughts....

Will She Anchor Deep?

_____

_____

_____

_____

_____

_____

_____

_____

_____

_____

_____

_____

_____

_____

_____

.... *shewill!!!*

Week 35

Romans 13:14 TPT

"Instead, fully immerse yourselves into the Lord Jesus, the Anointed One, and don't waste even a moment's thought on your former identity to awaken its selfish desires."

When we say yes to Jesus and we are saying, take me, change me, cleanse me and let me fall totally in love with Jesus.

This is when we start longing for and making a decision to fully immerse ourselves in Jesus. He is the anointed one, the one who came, lived, died, and rose again. We must let go of the past and allow God to take us deeper in him so we can shed off the old self and allow the Holy Spirit to renew our minds. It's so important to be baptized, when we immerse ourselves in the water we are submitting to the washing off the old and coming up new, reborn....

The battles that we face every day start in our minds. Our minds are the devil's playground if we allow him to come play. It's very important that we immerse ourselves in the Anointed One, Jesus. He has the answers and directions that we need. He's in the business of pulling down the strongholds that so easily beset us and conquering the evil one. Rom 12:2, be not conformed to this world: but be transformed by the renewing of your mind, 2 Co 10:4, the weapons of our warfare are not carnal, but mighty through God to the pulling down of strongholds.

It's just a simple fact, we alone cannot defeat the enemy, but with God by our side we can and will conquer. Not allowing the sinful desires to take over is a daily commitment. Think about this; when we were serving the devil (you might be saying I didn't serve the devil), well if you weren't serving God then you are serving the devil. He wasn't worried about you then, but now, serving God and desiring to be immersed in Jesus, the past constantly tries to creep in and get you off course. But when we stay under the blood and under the covering of God Almighty, not only can we win, but we have also won!

Once we say yes to Jesus, we have all of heaven fighting for us. We need to realize that there is no one that can stop us from totally immersing ourselves in the word of God, where we get our strength, except ourselves.

When we take the plunge into the word of God, we learn to dwell in the presence of the Almighty One and allow the Holy Spirit to fight off the enemy. This is where we will be an overcomer.

Will you immerse yourself in the word of the Lord?

Will She totally immerse in the Almighty God and his promises for her?

She Will!

Lord, we pray today that we will walk in the newness of life and through the saving power of our Lord and Savior Jesus Christ! Help us Lord to immerse ourselves in the Word of the Lord, shed the old self and realize that we are a new creation in and through you Jesus, for you have given us the power to overcome and be a powerhouse for you, a light in the darkness and a fire that will never burn out. God help us to totally immerse ourselves in you so I will not look back but move forward to the prize that is set before us. In your lovely name Jesus, we pray.

Bev

Your Thoughts....

Will She Anchor Deep?

_____

_____

_____

_____

_____

_____

_____

_____

_____

_____

_____

_____

_____

_____

.... shewill!!!

Week 36

Matthew 3:11 NIV

"I baptize you with water for repentance. But after me will come one who is more powerful than I, whose sandals I am not fit to carry. He will baptize you with the Holy Spirit and with fire."

Oh, dear sister! John is speaking of what he came to do as the forerunner to Jesus who would come to baptize us with His Holy Spirit and with fire! I don't know about you but that makes me jump for joy!!!! Jesus came to John to be baptized by water, a symbol of us dying to our old man and being born again in Christ. When Jesus came out of the water, heaven was opened! At this moment Jesus saw the Spirit of God descending like a dove and lighting on him. This is such a model of what would be given to us through God's Son to whom God's voice said, "This is my Son, whom I love; with him I am well pleased." How beautiful!

Before Jesus died, he told His disciples to go to the temple and wait for the Holy Spirit to come upon them. Through obedience, they were filled with the Holy Spirit and began to speak in other tongues as the Spirit enabled them. (Acts 2:4) The disciples after Jesus' death did not start the great commission of spreading the gospel until they received the Holy Spirit.

I did not grow up understanding the Holy Spirit, though I did grow up in church. My heart was God's; I was saved; Hallelujah! One day, a pastor I trusted ministered to me in my brokenness.

That day he took water from the Jordan River, anointed my head while praying over me, and baptized me in the Holy Spirit. I didn't understand it but I knew I needed all of God I could get.

Within two months I had my prayer language. A language that intercedes straight from the Holy Spirit to the throne of God cutting Satan out. I needed that! I think we all do. If you have not been baptized in the Holy Spirit and want to be, grab some anointing oil. Olive oil will do, put some on your finger and put a cross on your forehead. Repeat this prayer out loud.

Will She be filled with the Holy Spirit?

She Will!

I anoint myself in the name of the Father, Son, and Holy Spirit and with the power vested in me as Your daughter standing in agreement with my She Will Sisters, we baptize you in the Holy Spirit. Holy Spirit, Come! Fill me and release within me all that you have for me. Release my belly and my tongue with my heavenly prayer language, Father. Help me to stand in belief of all the power and authority that You have placed in me, in Jesus' name, Amen.

Sara

Your Thoughts….

Will She Anchor Deep?

_____
_____
_____
_____
_____
_____
_____
_____
_____
_____
_____
_____
_____
_____
_____
_____

…. shewill!!!

Week 37

Psalm 107:35

"He turns a wilderness into a pool of water, And a dry land into springs of water;"

We don't look forward to the wilderness experience. It is dry and hot, and we can do nothing to help ourselves there. Nothing to ease our suffering or anguish, or our confusion and hurt.

The wilderness is the place where we have shut out everyone, but God is waiting to meet with us in the dry places of our soul.

He has living water for us after our experience of dryness.

Our dry times will drive us to salvation. That's the place where we know we need to be saved and receive Jesus as Lord.

We feel undone and need to surrender to the Lord. We need to be saved. He alone will quench our thirst with living water.

John 7:38

"He who believes in Me, as the scripture has said, out of his heart will flow living water;"

After we are saved there are many experiences we will encounter, the wilderness being one of them. When we have wilderness experiences it will cause our spiritual ears to open, we begin to thirst, we seek to hear from the Lord through His word and truly become thankful for His gift of life.

The wilderness is the place where we will have to totally depend on the Lord. There is no other help, not from friends or family or the environment. Only Jesus is there.

While Jesus was on this earth, He knew where to get His help. He would go into the wilderness and talk to His Father.

Luke 5:16 says, "So He Himself often withdrew into the wilderness and prayed".

Jesus knew where and when to withdraw to the wilderness to gain strength and hear from the Father.

Sometimes we are driven there by circumstances in life.

We should know that when we are in the wilderness experience of life that Father is waiting to speak to us. To reveal things to us that we are blinded to. He will open our understanding, give us direction and place hope in our heart once again.

Isaiah 58:11

"The Lord will guide you continually, and satisfy your soul in drought, And strengthen your bones. You shall be like a watered garden, like a spring of water, whose waters do not fail."

Living water is flowing and moving, it is not stagnant, and still. Keep moving forward in the Lord. Living water will create life wherever it flows. (Think on this)

Beloved, embrace your wilderness experience, we are not to fear it, but know that Father is waiting for us, to speak with us, as we reach out to Him in prayer.

We will all go through our wilderness, that is the place where we grow up in the Lord. Our weakness is now turned to strength!

Will She meet with the Lord in the wilderness?

Will She allow the dry places to be filled with living water?

She Will!

Father God, thank you for your word that reminds us of your promises that turn our dry places into pools of fresh water. I invite you into the dry areas to bring your life into them. Make me like a well-watered garden. Open my understanding of how precious I am to You. Thank you, Lord, for all your protection, in every place I set my feet.

In Jesus name, Amen.

Joy

Your Thoughts....

Will She Anchor Deep?

_____

_____

_____

_____

_____

_____

_____

_____

_____

_____

_____

_____

_____

_____

_____

_____

_____

.... *shewill!!!*

Week 38

Isaiah 49:10 NIV

"They will neither hunger nor thirst, nor will the desert heat or the sun beat down on them. He who has compassion on them will guide them and lead them beside springs of water."

Have you ever felt dry and thirsty? What came to mind as you read that? A physical thirst, possibly from heat or exertion? Emotional thirst, where you have cried and cried until you feel that there are no tears left? What about spiritual thirst? A time where you feel disconnected from God, and from the fellowship with other believers? How do we respond in those times?

As a child in the 1970s, there was a commercial depicting thirsty children needing refreshment. No matter where they were, they could call out, "Hey, Kool–aid." All of a sudden, the music starts up, you hear, and you hear a loud, "Oh, yeah" as a large, smiling, glass pitcher filled with red beverage bursts through barriers to deliver his icy-cold liquid. The slogan: Kool-Aid's got thirst on the run. A few sips and they were instantly refreshed. Oh, if only it was that simple.

Remembering some of those parched places in my life, whether it was related to my job, marriage, chronic illness, or related to choices I had made which distanced me from God and from others, quick refreshment wasn't possible.

Have you ever had a living house plant? To keep it alive and healthy, it must be watered on a regular basis. This requires going to the source of water over and over again as often as we need to. Whether we are starting out really parched, or just need consistent hydration to be healthy, Jesus has compassion on us and will guide us and lead us besides springs of water.

We can trust that He will provide what we need, quenching our thirst over and over again.

Is Jesus your source?

When you are dry and thirsty, Will She anchor deep?

She Will!

Lord Jesus, You are living water. We can trust in You to provide for all our needs, to refresh and restore us. Help us to turn to You first as our source. Help us to trust, to believe, and to receive the provision that you have for us. In Jesus' name, Amen.

Laura Anne

Your Thoughts….

Will She Anchor Deep?

_____

_____

_____

_____

_____

_____

_____

_____

_____

_____

_____

_____

_____

_____

_____

_____

.... shewill!!!

Week 39

John 3:16 NIV

"For God so loved the world that He gave His one and only Son; that whoever believes in him should not perish but have eternal life."

Greatest Love Story.

I believe this one verse tells us more about God than any other in the Bible. I have always thought of the verse as a love statement. This is how much He loves us; He would give His Son to die for us and our sins. How much love is that?

I have a son that I love very much, but I can't think of a person in the world I would give my son up to die for. My love is just a worldly love of a mother. God loved us so much that He gave His Son to die on a cross for us. That kind of amazing sacrificial love is mind boggling! All He asks is that we confess our sinfulness; confess Him as our Savior and He gives us the gift of eternal life.

Have you ever written a love letter or received one? Think about that for a minute. How did it make you feel whether writing or receiving? It is an expression of love. The Bible is God's love letter to us. In this precious love letter, He tells us how much He loves us. God's love was so mighty that He gave His most precious gift...His Son for us. We need to shout this love from the rooftops.

Will She accept His love and receive the gift of eternal life?

She Will and God's love will anchor her!

Father, I cannot express how thankful I am for your free gift of eternity spent with you. I am humbled that you would sacrifice your son to pay for my sins. I know that I am a sinner, and I ask for Your forgiveness. I believe You died for my sins and rose from the dead. I turn from my sins and invite You to come into my heart and life. I make you my Lord and my Savior. Amen.

Jo Ann

Your Thoughts….

Will She Anchor Deep?

_____

_____

_____

_____

_____

_____

_____

_____

_____

_____

_____

_____

_____

_____

_____

_____

.... shewill!!!

Week 40

Ezekiel 47:3 NIV

"As the man went eastward with a measuring line in his hand, he measured off a thousand cubits and then led me through water that was ankle-deep."

It is with such joy that I share the vision of She Will Conference with you, but before I can continue, please read Ezekiel 47:1-12.

These verses were brought to my attention by the Lord at the same time He dropped the She Will Conference into my spirit in July of 2017. I revisit these verses every year to remind myself what God was (and is) telling me and every time He reestablishes the vision and reveals more depth of meaning. God is so gracious as He reveals truth to us. He allows us to live it, sit in it, grow, and transform to it.

I knew in 2017 that the depth levels of the river represented our walking, talking relationship with Christ. Some are ankle deep, new believers or baby Christians. While others have measured out. They have dug a bit deeper, lived through more experiences, sought the Lord, and are knee deep in their walk. Still there are those who hunger and thirst for more, witness the goodness of God and when they seek the Lord, they find themselves waist deep. It is harder to walk in water that is waist deep compared to ankle deep. The Living Water weighs more, you begin to truly feel Him all around you. Every move reminds you of His presence. And yet you know there is abundantly more than you can ask or imagine. Now that you have tasted and seen that the Lord is good you become brave and ask what Moses asked, "Let me see your glory". You measure out once more because nothing else can satisfy. When we desire only Christ, His ways, His glory, His presence, it is then we are immersed in the river of living water. I have been crucified with Christ. The life I now live is in Him. No longer able to walk but now swimming!

This river is the gospel of Jesus Christ powered by the Holy Spirit. When we are steeped in the river of life and our paths cross those who are in salty water, we will be instruments of healing! The scriptures say that wherever this river flows, everything will flourish and bear fruit.

When you think about the four levels of water depth; ankle, knee, waist, and over your head, where do you see yourself? There is no wrong answer. We are where we are, but Jesus is asking us to measure out (trust) and take a step deeper into the water.

I want to encourage you to get out in the deep. This is where the great adventure finds you. I call this the "God Zone".

Will She measure out?

Will She take a step deeper in?

She Will!

Lord, show me where I am in this river. Am I ankle deep? Am I knee deep? Do I need to measure out? I am waist deep? Am I in the 'God Zone" where it is so deep that I can only trust you to carry me? Teach me how to be brave, how to move forward. I want the great adventure with you!

In Jesus name, Amen.

Shelsea

Your Thoughts….

Will She Anchor Deep?

_____

_____

_____

_____

_____

_____

_____

_____

_____

_____

_____

_____

_____

.... shewill!!!

Week 41

James 1:6 KJV

"But let him ask in faith, nothing wavering. For he that wavereth is like a wave of the sea driven with the wind and tossed."

Years ago, when asked to share my testimony in a Youth Group, I felt awkward. My testimony did not include a life-altering event that led me to accept Jesus as my savior. Instead, I had always believed in Him. At that moment, I felt embarrassed by the lack of an intriguing story. But now, looking back, I realize that my testimony of a long-time belief in Jesus is simply a strong testimony of faith.

Faith is the belief in something that we cannot see. As Christians, we believe in a God that we cannot physically see. Therefore, we rely on the Bible and the Holy Spirit to reveal glimpses of God. We can, then, see evidence of His qualities, characteristics, and majesty in the world around us.

However, since we do not get to see Jesus like the 12 disciples used to, we can easily feel disheartened. This is when we must buckle up and stand firm in our faith. We need to remember all that God has done for us, how He has provided for us, and all He has promised He will do.

A strong faith will prepare you for times of hardship. Because of the faith you have grown and built up, you will be able to come before the Lord and ask of Him. Believe that God will come through for you. Go ahead and ask. Lay it out all in front of Him. Do not waver but be strong and confident. Be confident in what you believe!

Faith has proved to be incredibly important in my own life. I know firsthand the pain of allowing doubt to creep in and demolish faith. We cannot allow the devil to separate us from the love of our Father! So, build up a faith that is strong and unwavering, a faith that will survive all the storms life throws at you.

Will She build up an unwavering faith?

Yes, She Will!

Dear Heavenly Father,

Thank you for being present in my life even though I cannot physically see you. Thank you for revealing yourself to me. Please continue showing me your ways. Remind me of all that you have done and provided for me. May I never forget your love, forgiveness, help, and protection.

Instill in me a faith that will survive storms. Thank you! Amen.

Savanna

Your Thoughts....

Will She Anchor Deep?

... shewill!!!

Week 42

Psalms 51:7 NIV

"Cleanse me with hyssop, and I will be clean; wash me, and I will be whiter than snow."

What is Hyssop?

Here's a fun fact: Every time we see the hyssop plant in the Old Testament it is connected to a ritual dealing with cleansing or forgiving sin. It is used in Leviticus 14:4-7 with the blood in the ceremonial cleansing for the leper. It is used in Numbers 19:1 for cleaning someone who has touched a dead body. It was the plant Israel used at the first Passover as a paintbrush to paint the blood of the Passover lamb over the door post.

Exodus 12:22 (ESV): 22 Take a bunch of hyssops and dip it in the blood that is in the basin, touch the lintel and the two doorposts with the blood that is in the basin. None of you shall go out of the door of his house until the morning.

It is the plant David was talking about when he said cleanse me with Hyssop.

Psalm 51:7 (ESV): 7 Purge me with hyssop, and I shall be clean; wash me, and I shall be whiter than snow.

When Jesus was on the cross in His final moments He asked for a drink. The Roman's soldier took a hyssop plant and put a sponge on the end, dipped it in vinegar (representing God's wrath that we were supposed to drink) and put it to his lips. The Hyssop plant is used to connect us with the fact that Jesus was finishing His mission, He was taking our sin and cleansing us. Jesus our Savior who washes us clean, making us whiter than snow.

John 19:29–30 (KJV 1900): 29 Now there was set a vessel full of vinegar: and they filled a sponge with vinegar, and put it upon hyssop, and put it to his mouth. 30 When Jesus therefore had received the vinegar, he said, it is finished: and he bowed his head, and gave up the ghost.

We are all like David, a sinner in need of a Savior. What a beautiful reminder that we have in our Lord Jesus. We must honor His sacrifice, there is a reason on the first Passover that they did not put the Passover lamb's blood on the threshold, because the blood was not meant to be stepped on. When we Live in a state of habitual sin, we do just that. Let us live lives that honor the sacrifice Jesus made for us. Let us live Holy lives as unto God.

Are we living lives that honor Christ and his sacrifice?

Will She live a life honoring Him?

She Will!

Dear Lord, help me remember what you did for me on the cross. When I lose my way cleanse me with the hyssop plant, and if I step on your blood swat me with it like a switch. I love you Lord and I honor you. I was just kidding about the switch. Well Kind of.

In Christ Name

Victoria

Your Thoughts….

Will She Anchor Deep?

_____

_____

_____

_____

_____

_____

_____

_____

_____

_____

_____

_____

_____

_____

.... shewill!!!

Week 43

Matthew 14:29-40 NIV

"Then Peter got down out of the boat, walked on the water and came toward Jesus. But when he saw the wind, he was afraid and, beginning to sink, cried out, 'Lord, save me!'"

The disciples have been sailing all night. As dawn approaches, Jesus decides it is time to join them. As they near their destination on the far shore of the Sea of Galilee, what do they see behind them? Jesus, whom they had left behind to spend some alone time with His Father.

Jesus had walked the entire length of the body of water they had just spent hours sailing across in order to catch up to them! How could that be? How could Jesus have walked on top of swirling waves for 3 to 4 miles?!

The disciples felt shocked and afraid. They did not understand what was happening before their very eyes. But when Jesus tells Peter to take courage and not be afraid, Peter instantly trusts that familiar voice. In fact, Peter trusts Jesus so much he gets down out of the boat to go to Jesus! That is faith!

As long as he fixes his gaze on Jesus, Peter, too, is able to walk on the thrashing water. But when Peter takes his eyes off his Savior and begins to look at his circumstances–the wind–the disciple begins to sink.

It wasn't that the wind suddenly kicked up, scaring Peter. The wind was swirling all around him before he decided to get out of the boat; the wind was howling when Peter walked successfully atop the water; the wind blew when Peter began to sink.

The wind did not change. What changed? Peter began to sink when he took his eyes off Jesus and began to look around at his dangerous, terrifying, overwhelming circumstances.

As long as he was "anchored" to the Savior, Peter felt safe and successfully navigated difficult circumstances. But when he took his focus off Jesus, Peter lost his way. His "anchor" was uprooted, and he began to falter.

Like Peter we must fix our eyes on Jesus, the author and perfecter of our faith, if we want to weather life's storms faithfully. We must "anchor" ourselves to Christ through the scriptures, devoting ourselves to spending intentional time with our Lord in prayer and worship.

Will She anchor deep?

She Will!

Father, we thank you that we have access to You through Your Son, Jesus Christ. We confess we are easily distracted by our circumstances. We so often fail to keep our eyes fixed on Jesus.

And when our attention turns to the left or to the right, we begin to sink. Lord, anchor us deeply in the truth of Your Word and in Your love, that we might have a steady gaze on You–our protector, our provider, our Lord. In the name of Jesus we pray, Amen!

Kelly

Your Thoughts….

Will She Anchor Deep?

_____

_____

_____

_____

_____

_____

_____

_____

_____

_____

_____

_____

_____

_____

_____

_____

.... *shewill!!!*

Week 44

Psalms 51:2 NIV

"Wash me thoroughly from my iniquity and cleanse me from my sin."

Do you sometimes feel like you're drowning in shame or guilt? For me it is spending enough time on the Bible. I want to know it inside and out. That word busy comes up and before too long we are lucky to get in the verse of the day much less reading the word. I was at a conference not long ago, and we had some one-on-one time with a prayer partner that we did not know. The lady that I was paired with taught me something that reminds me to check myself. B U S Y is an acronym for: Being Under Satan's Yoke. I know who is cleansing me from my sins, and I also know who is trying to attack at every corner. We cannot even fathom the grace God gives us.

God reminds us in this verse He is there to wash and cleanse you from all your sin. Next time you find yourself saying the word busy, ask yourself why? Are you putting too much on your plate, or is the devil trying to intercede?

Will She let the grace of God CLEANSE her?

She Will!

Lord, I thank you for always being there for me when my flesh tells me I can't go on, you remind me I can. I thank you for cleansing my heart when evil tries to step in. Please help to be more like you God and less of me, in Jesus' name, Amen.

Dawn

Your Thoughts....

Will She Anchor Deep?

_____

_____

_____

_____

_____

_____

_____

_____

_____

_____

_____

_____

_____

_____

_____

.... *shewill!!!*

Week 45

Revelation 7:14 NKJV

"I answered, "Sir, you know."

And he said, "These are they who have come out of the great tribulation; they have washed their robes and made them white in the blood of the Lamb."

You know that feeling when someone important and powerful calls on you with a question, but you don't have the answer? That is what John was facing in Revelation 7. "Who are they and where did they come from?" That was the question, from the elder. John did not know. He spent three years with Jesus. He was in the Lord's inner circle and could not begin to understand the multitudes of worshippers he was being shown, Revelation 7:9, 13. All John could do was answer respectfully, "I don't know, but you do."

At the beginning of his Gospel, John records a different John, John the Baptist declaring Jesus was the lamb who takes away the sins of the world, John 1:29. Suddenly, the apostle was faced with the reality of those saved spiritually by that Lamb and physically destroyed, during a time of unparalleled persecution and suffering, the Great Tribulation.

It is an odd thing to follow a lamb. They have no roar or howl. Lambs do not attack. They walk towards sacrifice. The white-robed multitude follow Him to the point of laying down their lives.

Despite what we often hear, many face trials far beyond the ability to endure, 2 Corinthians 1:8-9. Through their anguish, they trust in Him. When their broken bodies can withstand no more, they will be welcomed into His presence, Revelation 7:15.

Turning to Christ, during the tribulation, the saints clothed in white followed the lamb to the end.

Devotion costs them everything including their lives. They lived the promise; the one who endures to the end will be saved, Matthew 24:13. Only the blood of the Lamb, Jesus, can make us clean. Only He can clothe us in holiness and purity. However, steadfastness sustains believers, in impossible times, 1 Peter 5:6-10, Revelation 14:11-12.

Someday, their faithfulness will be rewarded, and their suffering avenged, 2 Samuel 22: 25-28.

When they see Jesus, the martyrs in the heavenly congregation will never hunger or thirst again, Isaiah 49:10, Revelation 7:16. Springs of living water will quench their thirst, Revelation 7:17. The Lord will wipe every tear from their eyes, Isaiah 25:8, Revelation 7:17. Eventually, those who endure will understand all the hurt, all the torment, all the travail this world can offer will be worth it, when we see Jesus, 2 Corinthians 4:17. Until then, we can face uncertain times saying, "Lord, I don't know, but you do."

Will She endure until the end?

She Will!

Lord, you are the God who sees and understands everything. Thank you for shedding your blood to cleanse us. Guide us through uncertain times. Give us wisdom. Give us strength. Give us the confidence to say, "Lord I don't know what is happening, but you do."

Julie

Your Thoughts….

Will She Anchor Deep?

_____

_____

_____

_____

_____

_____

_____

_____

_____

_____

_____

_____

_____

_____

_____

…. shewill!!!

Week 46

Mark 4:39 NIV

"He got up, rebuked the wind, and said to the waves, "Quiet! Be still!" Then the wind died down and it was completely calm."

By the time we get to this verse in Mark Jesus is already asleep... Most likely He was worn out from an exhausting day with what I like to call "People-ing!" He has dealt with massive crowds all day, so by the end of the day Jesus says to His disciples in verse 35 "Let us go over to the other side." Probable translation, "I need a break guys!"

But wouldn't you know life crashes in on them in a big way; the Bible says the disciples were terrified! Waves crash against the boat, tossing it to and fro...sea water pouring in on them threatening to sink them and destroy any likelihood of making it to shore safely, and the noise! I can't imagine how frightening the sounds of the lightning and thunder must have been, causing them to rush to Jesus in dismay, "Teacher! Don't you care if we drown?"

And then we read our key verse. But wait... next we see His surprising response to the disciples; He turns and rebukes them as well! Why would He scold them for being afraid in this violent storm? When chaos is swirling around you and you're unsure of your circumstances, questioning everything...who wouldn't be afraid and maybe even accuse God of not caring?

Look again to verse 35...He tells them, "We are going to the other side." Period. He doesn't say unless we get sidetracked by a violent storm. He has already told them what will happen, and where they are going...yet when the storm pops up they are all afraid for their lives.

How many times do we do that? Default to doubt and fear even though over and over and over in His Word God tells us things like He will never leave us or forsake us. He has told us there is nothing that can separate us from His love... and Psalm 91 is my absolute favorite chapter in the Bible because He didn't leave anything out, no room for doubting His ability and assurance that as Christ-followers we are safe under the wings of His protection.

Yes, storms in life will hit us, sometimes with brute force. But God has said I'm taking you to the other side and either we believe Him or not. We don't get to pick and choose our verses based upon where we are in a storm...God is faithful ALL the time!

Is there a storm in your life today?

Will She trust Him?

She Will!

Father, you are the Sovereign God; the master of all of Heaven and earth...and nothing can prevent me from accomplishing all that You have for me when I submit myself to your will. Lead me and guide me, cause faith to rise up in me so that I will not fear. In Jesus's name, Amen.

Liz

Your Thoughts....

Will She Anchor Deep?

.... shewill!!!

Week 47

John 14:27 NIV

"Peace, I leave with you; my peace I give you. I do not give to you as the world gives. Do not let your hearts be troubled and do not be afraid."

The beginning of this chapter opens with, "Do not let your hearts be troubled." Now that's not easy. If you watch any television, listen to any radio or noisy neighbor, you hear about all the troubles in this world. Actually, we're promised trouble; "In this world you will have trouble," "In the last days perilous times will come," Life is a few days of trouble" (Jn 16:33; 2 Tim 3:1; Job 14:1). The good news is there's a clause. "[Jesus] has overcome the world." He will rescue you and overpower our enemy.

The Psalmist David said he had lived a long life and as he reflected back, "he had never seen the righteous forsaken or God's seed begging for bread (Ps 37:25, KJV). The apostle Paul actually boasts about his 'troubles' of imprisonment, floggings, beatings with rods and whips, stoning's, shipwrecks, bandits, liars, hunger, thirst, coldness and nakedness, not to mention his concerns for the church (2 Cor 11:23-28). What David and Paul knew was the overcoming power of the Lord. That it is actually in our human weakness, when we're spent and no more wherewithal to continue, that HIS strength is manifested! His grace is sufficient for_____fill in the blank.

Recently, I was making a 600 plus mile trip in the middle of a storm path. You know when the storm tracker radar shows green, yellow, orange, and red, with red being the worst of the storm?

I was driving in the orange and red. But I had a secret weapon, prayer. My 84 y/o dad was also tracking the storm and praying for his daughter's safety. So, while the view from my windshield was minimal and trucks were crowding me off the interstate and spraying my car with even more oil and water, I had peace. I prayed, sang, listened to worship, and preached. While the storm was raging around me, inside that Lincoln MKZ, I had a little bit of heaven.

What storms or troubles are you facing today? Woman of God, be of good cheer, for Jesus has overcome all these things. His strength is manifested in your weakness and his grace is sufficient. So don't be troubled or afraid, but rather, rest in his peace.

Will you rest in his presence?

Will She have peace?

She Will!

Oh Jesus, thank you for your peace in troubled times. It doesn't make sense, and the world doesn't understand it. When all around us there are heart's failing, our heart is confident in you.

I receive your peace today and rest confidently in you.

Thresa

Your Thoughts….

Will She Anchor Deep?

_____

_____

_____

_____

_____

_____

_____

_____

_____

_____

_____

_____

_____

_____

_____

.... *shewill!!!*

Week 48

Psalms 145:18-20 NIV

"The Lord is close to all who call on him, yes, to all who call on him in truth."

Where have you placed your anchor today? Have you placed your hope in the world? Have you anchored in the Lord? Are you staying close to Him, keeping your heart open to the leading of the Lord? He desires to be close to us. He longs to have communion with his children every day. Do you feel like the Lord is close to you today or does he feel a million miles away?

There are times I've felt a million miles away from the Lord, I must take a minute and look to see who's moved; me or Him. When I take time to dwell in his presence, I hear his voice say.

"Come this way, for you have strayed, take my hand and I'll lead you back home" Jesus loves us more than we can fathom. His word tells us if we come to him with a humble heart, with all our brokenness and call out to him and lay our burdens down and He will answer. When we come to Jesus with a humble heart, ask him to clean us and take us deeper in him, He will not turn us away. He knows the very intent of our hearts, be it true or deceitful.

Vs 17 says God is incontestably, INDISPUTABLE. This says that God gives us a promise, we can take it to the bank. We need to draw close, anchor our soul in his promises then he can fulfill them in us.

Ps: 34 says that God is ever close to those who are broken hearted. He feels our pain and our joy. When we feel like everything and everyone is against us, it's not easy to say, "I'll trust you." God's word tells us He is the potter, and we are the clay. Allow Him to mold you into the beautiful masterpiece of his making.

All boats have an anchor. It keeps the boat from moving further than the line it is connected to.

It keeps the boat from drifting into the rocks or other obstacles. If we get anchored deep in Jesus, God gives us a lifeline that anchors our souls to him, that is our prayer language to communicate with the father. He has given us the tools to anchor in the right place, which is his word, his promises, and his truth. In James 4, he tells us to draw nigh to the Lord and He will draw nigh to us. It also tells us not to be double minded. There are promises God has given us so we can place our anchor and not waiver when the winds of life come. It keeps us from drifting too far from our dwelling place in him. Staying Anchored in God's word will keep the joy of the Lord alive in you and in the days of trouble you will have great peace in your walk with Jesus.

Will you go deeper in your walk with the Lord today?

Will She anchor deep?

She Will!

Lord, we come to you today with grateful hearts and with joy in our souls, knowing that your promises are indisputable. Help us today to dive deeper in your word that will bring the increase of your love to an overflowing spring of living water that will never run dry. Help me Lord to Anchor deep in you every day till the day we see you face to face. Amen.

Bev

Your Thoughts....

Will She Anchor Deep?

_____

_____

_____

_____

_____

_____

_____

_____

_____

_____

_____

_____

_____

_____

_____

.... *shewill!!!*

Week 49

Jeremiah 29:12 NIV

"Then you will call upon me and come and pray to me, and I will listen to you."

Verse 10 begins with, "This is what the Lord says..." He says that we will call upon Him, come and pray to Him, and He will listen to us. Notice the word will. He will listen to us. The Lord also doesn't say, "If we call upon Him." He is talking to His children which is who we are, grafted in by the blood of the lamb. His believers will call upon Him, come and pray to Him, and He will listen.

Do you go to your prayer closet with the faith that our Savior hears your voice? He does. He hears every prayer, every plea, every petition, and He listens to you. He loves you, He cares for you, right where you are. Sister, I don't know what's happening in your life today, but I know the One who does. He is with you, and He is for you. He will never leave you, nor forsake you.

These are His promises to all who believe. If you believe Jesus died on the Cross for your sins and that he rose again three days later to ascend to the right hand of His Father, then you are His child. He tells us to come to Him and call upon Him. Pray to Him, and He will listen.

What are you praying for today? A spouse to come to know Him? Prodigal family members to come home? Maybe it's sickness to leave you or a loved one? Whatever it may be, take it to your Heavenly Father who cares for your every need. If you don't have the words, then ask Him to give them to you. He will! Also, know that we are standing in agreement with you as sisters in Christ as you call upon our Father. What a good, good Father we have. He is Jehovah Jireh, the God that provides.

Will She call upon Him and believe He listens?

She Will!

Father, we come to you as sisters in Christ, and we stand in agreement with our sister. We ask that you meet her right where she is. We ask that she can see herself crawling on Your lap, resting her head on Your bosom, and You wrapping Your ever capable arms around her. You know everything about her Father, every need she has, and the needs of those she loves. Help her to call upon you, come and pray to you, and help her to know You are listening, in Jesus' name, Amen.

Sara

Your Thoughts....

Will She Anchor Deep?

_____

_____

_____

_____

_____

_____

_____

_____

_____

_____

_____

_____

_____

_____

.... shewill!!!

Week 50

Jeremiah 17:7,8 NIV

"But blessed is the one who trusts in the LORD, whose confidence is in him. They will be like a tree planted by the water that sends out its roots by the stream. It does not fear when heat comes; its leaves are always green. It has no worries in a year of drought and never fails to bear fruit."

Remember the old song, count your blessings, name them one by one, thanking God for all He has done?

Blessed people are people who know their God and hear His voice and follow Him.

We receive God's blessing by grace. He bestows divine favor (grace) on those that are in Christ Jesus and follow Him.

When we have faith in Jesus Christ and walk in His love, blessings will follow us everywhere we go. Psalm 23:6 (Read all of 23, you probably know it by heart, but concentrate on each word)

Starting with The Lord Is my shepherd. I shall not want. Verse 6. Surely goodness and mercy shall follow me All the days of my life; And I will dwell in the house of the Lord forever.

Goodness and mercy are all blessings in our life from the Lord. This is a promise from the word of God. There are 3000 promises in God's word. They are there to show us what blessings we have in the Lord.

Blessings bring us happiness, in fact the word means, happy and to be envied. Jesus gives us great joy, but our blessings give us happiness.

The abundant life is not necessarily a lot of stuff, but surely, all the provision we will need. Life does not consist in the abundance of things. (Luke 12:15)

2 Corinthians 9:8 (A blessing)

"And God is able to make all grace abound toward you, that you, always having all sufficiency for every good work."

Philippians 4:19 (A Blessing and promise)

"And my God shall supply all your needs according to His riches in glory by Christ Jesus."

Psalm 138:7 (A blessing and a promise)

Though I walk in the midst of trouble, You will revive me; You stretch out Your hand Against the wrath of my enemies, And Your right hand will save me.

Beloved, we are so blessed of God, He has poured out on us every spiritual blessing as well as provided for our natural blessings. Like, food, shelter, clothing, and great relationships with those that are like minded. These all provide for us happiness. They make our hearts glad.

We have so many blessings, all we must do is look around. Be thankful to God for our great inheritance that we have in Jesus Christ.

So, count your blessings, name them one by one, and praise God for all He has done and is doing. Jesus Christ, the same, yesterday, today, and forever.

Will She count her blessings?

She Will!

Father, I want to always be the one that turns back to say Thank You. Thank you for every one of my blessings. They are more numerous than the stars. I see that I am blessed and highly favored by you, your grace and by your mercy. May I be a blessing to the people you have placed in my life.

In Jesus' name, Amen.

Joy

Your Thoughts….

Will She Anchor Deep?

_____

_____

_____

_____

_____

_____

_____

_____

_____

_____

_____

_____

_____

_____

_____

_____

.... *shewill!!!*

Week 51

1 Peter 2:4-5 NIV

"As you come to him, the living Stone – rejected by humans but chosen by God and precious to him- you also, like living stones, are being built into a spiritual house to be a holy priesthood, offering spiritual sacrifices acceptable to God through Jesus Christ."

I grew up in a time, in a place, where you didn't ask if people were Christians- instead, assuming that they were, you asked where they went to church. There were numerous nearby choices, representing different denominational beliefs and styles of worship. It was rare that someone did not name a particular church building, even if they only attended at Christmas and Easter. This verse teaches the fallacy of that thinking. We didn't GO to church; we ARE the church.

When Jesus was alive people went to the temple in Jerusalem to worship. According to the Holman Illustrated Bible dictionary, the temple was usually referred to as the "House of God" because He [God] is said to have dwelled there. In that day, the temple was described as a magnificent stone structure, purposefully constructed to carry out the service of the priests. If you have ever constructed a house, you know the importance of a solid, firm foundation to the long-term stability of the structure. Jesus is the foundational corner – stone, the strong solid basis of our faith, our Anchor.

As living stones, we are the spiritual house, meaning that the Holy Spirit lives in us. Several verses speak to this including Ephesians 2:22, "And in Him, you too are being built together to become a dwelling in which God lives by His Spirit." While it is important to fellowship with other believers, where padded seats in a climate-controlled building make that more comfortable, it's not the wood, brick, metal, or stone buildings that define the church- it's the people of God.

Prior to the sacrifice of Jesus's shed blood on the cross for the forgiveness of our sins, animal sacrifices were offered for without the shedding of blood, there is no forgiveness (Hebrews 9:22). Now, we are to offer "spiritual sacrifices." What does that look like? Romans 12:1 urges us to offer our bodies as a living sacrifice, holy and pleasing to God – this is your spiritual act of worship. The Holman dictionary says, "Biblical elements of worship include prayer, praise, thanksgiving, charity/giving, confession, preaching and teaching, the reading of Scripture, and discipline."

Will She allow Christ to be the cornerstone, the anchor of her faith?

Will She please God through worship and spiritual sacrifices?

She Will!

Lord, when church buildings stood empty during the COVID pandemic, we were reminded that, as believers, we are your dwelling place, called to offer spiritual sacrifices to You. Please show each of us how to serve you, helping us to grow in all of the various elements of worship. We know that in Christ, we can stand firm in our faith, and to boldly serve you. Amen.

Laura Anne

Brand, C., Draper, C., England, A., Bond, S., Clendenen, R. R., & Butler, T.C. (Eds.) (2003). Holman Illustrated Bible Dictionary. Holman Bible Publishers.

Your Thoughts....

Will She Anchor Deep?

_____

_____

_____

_____

_____

_____

_____

_____

_____

_____

_____

_____

_____

_____

.... shewill!!!

Week 52

Deuteronomy 32:4 NIV

"He is the Rock, his works are perfect, and all his ways are just. A faithful God who does no wrong, upright and just is he."

The Rock

As a family, we were in New Mexico doing some hiking. Someone mentioned doing some small mountain climbing. Going mountain climbing had never been on my bucket list! I do not like heights. As we started, I grabbed each rock as if it was my lifeline. As we went a little higher, I grabbed a rock that I could wrap my arms around. I hung on for dear life. Are you picturing this?

I knew as long as I held on, that rock would keep me steady. My faith was in that rock to hold me steady.

Look up the definition of rock…solid. When times are difficult for us, who do we cling to? Who or what do we grab a hold of? Do we sometimes go to friends, family, pastor, counselor, or retail therapy? None of these are bad necessarily, but the scripture tells us God is "the" rock. He needs to be the first one we go to.

The above scripture tells us God is our Rock and He is faithful. In life circumstances I want to grab a hold of a rock that is faithful and will steady me. I cling to that Rock in this crazy world.

God is a just God who does no wrong. He makes no mistakes. He is a solid Rock. He won't lose ground and roll down a mountain like a regular rock might. He is firm and secure.

God's Word is there for us, to guide us, to help us with any situation we might be going through.

His works are perfect.

Will She dig deep in the Word and cling to the Rock?

She Will!

Father God, my Rock ..thank you for being a stronghold in my life. As I pray "your will", I know your will is steadfast and perfect. What perfection! I cling to you as I walk through this life of mine with so many unknowns. Thank you for loving me so very much. Amen.

Jo Ann

Your Thoughts….

Will She Anchor Deep?

_____

_____

_____

_____

_____

_____

_____

_____

_____

_____

_____

_____

_____

_____

_____

_____

_____

_____

_____

_____

.... *shewill!!!*